I Don't Want to Go to College

DATE DUE

I Don't Want to Go to College

Other Paths to Success

Heather Z. Hutchins ▶

an imprint of the American Library Association

HURON STREET PRESS

CHICAGO • 2013

Published by Huron Street Press, an imprint of ALA Publishing
Printed in the United States of America
17 16 15 14 13   5 4 3 2 1

Extensive effort has gone into ensuring the reliability of the information in this book; however, the publisher makes no warranty, express or implied, with respect to the material contained herein.

ISBNs: 978-1-937589-01-1 (paper); 978-1-937589-31-8 (PDF); 978-1-937589-32-5 (ePub); 978-1-937589-33-2 (Kindle). For more information on digital formats, visit the ALA Store at alastore.ala.org and select eEditions.

Library of Congress Cataloging-in-Publication Data
Hutchins, Heather Z.
  I don't want to go to college : other paths to success / Heather Z. Hutchins.
     p. cm.
  Includes bibliographical references and index.
  ISBN 978-1-937589-01-1 (pbk. : alk. paper) 1. Vocational guidance. 2. Vocational education. 3. Occupational training. I. Title.
  HF5381.H88 2013
  650.1—dc23
                                                                        2012003394

Series book design in Liberation Serif, Union, and Soho Gothic by Casey Bayer
Cover image © Pan Xunbin/Shutterstock, Inc.

♾ This paper meets the requirements of ANSI/NISO Z39.48-1992 (Permanence of Paper).

Contents

Preface   vii

1 ▶ **It's All about You**
Finding Your Skills and Interests and Exploring the Job Landscape   1

2 ▶ **Jobs without Formal Training**
Learning on the Job   19

3 ▶ **Jobs with Formal Training**
Where Apprenticeships and Specialized Training Can Take You   41

4 ▶ **Jobs with a Certificate**
Where Credentials Can Take You   55

5 ▶ **Jobs with an Associate Degree**
Where Two Years of College Can Take You   65

6 ▶ **Getting the Training and Education You Need**
Where Should You Look?   75

7 ▶ **Applications and Essays**
How to Succeed   85

8 ▶ **Resumes**
Showing Them What You Know   97

9 ▶ **Interviewing**
How to Be Likable   111

10 ▶ **Paying for Training and Education**
Estimating Costs and Applying for Financial Aid   125

Resources   151

Index   177

Preface

According to the Project on Student Debt, a nonprofit independent research and policy organization, most students pay for their four-year college degree by taking out loans. In 2010, the average debt for graduating seniors with student loans rose to $25,250, up more than a third from 2004.[1] And the number of students going into debt to go to college is increasing:

> ▶ In 2010, two-thirds of students who graduated from four-year colleges and universities borrowed money for school; in 1993, fewer than half borrowed money to pay for school.[2]
>
> ▶ In 2008, 84 percent of undergraduates had credit cards, compared to 67 percent in 1998.[3] In 2008, seniors with credit cards graduated with an average credit card debt of more than $4,100, up 41 percent from 2004, and 92 percent of undergraduates with credit cards said they used their cards to pay an education expense.[4]

In addition, college costs continue to rise. The average cost of tuition and fees for public four-year colleges and universities, even adjusted for inflation, has more than tripled in the last three decades, and it looks as if this trend will continue.[5]

It's no wonder that many students are deciding that college is not for them. In fact, it doesn't have to be. There are other paths to a successful career. The following chapters cover all of the steps to finding a path that works for you.

As you read, you will see that there are many training and education options that will widen your range of opportunities if you have no desire to attend a four-year college or university. Even if you don't want to attend a four-year college, you will most likely want to receive some additional training or education eventually. The average unemployment rate in 2011 for people with only a high school education was about 9.4 percent, but for individuals with some education and no degree, this number falls to 8.7 percent. For those with a two-year associate degree, the unemployment rate drops to 6.8 percent. Pay follows a similar pattern in reverse, with salary increasing the more training and education people receive.[6]

Luckily, you have many options. Apprenticeship programs offer training for jobs that are projected to grow faster through 2020 than jobs you can get with any other education or training level.[7] And with apprenticeship programs, you are typically paid for your training.

Keep an open mind as you read this book. If none of the jobs profiled in these pages appeals to you, you can use the career exploration tools in chapter 1 to find some that do.

Good luck with your career search! You are already taking a good first step.

Notes

1. Project on Student Debt, "Average Student Debt Tops $25,000 for Class of 2010 in Tough Job Market," news release, November 3, 2011 (http://projectonstudentdebt.org).
2. Andrew Martin and Andrew W. Lehren, "A Generation Hobbled by the Soaring Cost of College," *New York Times*, May 12, 2012, www.nytimes.com/2012/05/13/business/student-loans-weighing -down-a-generation-with-heavy-debt.html.
3. Sallie Mae Foundation, *How Undergraduate Students Use Credit Cards: Sallie Mae's National Study of Usage Rates and Trends 2009* (Wilkes-Barre, PA: Sallie Mae Foundation, 2009), 5.
4. Ibid., 8, 11.
5. College Board, *Trends in College Pricing 2011*, Trends in Higher Education Series, College Board Advocacy and Policy Center,

2011. Full report available at http://trends.collegeboard.org/
college_pricing.

6. U.S. Department of Labor, Bureau of Labor Statistics, "Education
    Pays," *Current Population Survey*, 2011. Available at www.bls.gov/
    emp/ep_chart_001.htm.

7. U.S. Department of Labor, Bureau of Labor Statistics, *Employment
    Projections—2010–2020 Summary*, February 1, 2012. Available at
    http://bls.gov/news.release/ecopro.nr0.htm.

ONE

It's All about You

Finding Your Skills and Interests and Exploring the Job Landscape

Some people are lucky enough to be born knowing exactly what they want to "be"—what they would like to do as a career. For the rest of us, figuring out what we want is more of a journey. Depending on your attitude, the journey can be an adventure with fun along the way or a scary trek through very dark woods. Don't worry. With just a little effort on your part, you can find many possible career options that you will enjoy and that will make you a living wage.

This chapter covers the five primary ways to find career possibilities that suit your interests:

- Talking to professional career counselors
- Exploring what kinds of jobs are out there
- Taking career and personality assessment tests
- Conducting informational interviews
- Taking an inventory of your strengths and interests

In all five, the most important skills are the ability to ask questions and keep an open mind about the careers all around you. Especially in the early stages of your search, do not limit yourself to obvious choices.

Move a little further afield to look at unusual jobs, jobs around the country or around the world, and jobs in emerging fields.

Meet with a Career Counselor

One good way to figure out your preferred career is to talk to a professional career counselor, such as your high school guidance counselor or a counselor at a local college career center, at a private firm, or with a local or federal jobs program. Career counselors are trained to assist you in figuring out your job and life goals. Talking through your interests with a professional will narrow the scope of your career search.

High School Counselor

If you are still in high school or are a recent graduate, the easiest start is to visit your high school counselor and ask for advice. Most high school counselors are trained to help students figure out their career interests. Sometimes the counselor will just talk to you. Sometimes you'll get brochures or computer printouts. And sometimes you'll find yourself sitting at a computer either taking a career assessment test or looking up jobs that sound interesting in a career database. One of the big advantages to talking to your high school counselor is that it's free. Most of the career testing offered by this type of counselor is free, too.

Local College Career Center

The two- and four-year colleges in your area will almost certainly have career centers. In many cases, career center staff will help community members with their career searches for a small fee. If you didn't get enough help from your high school counselor, or if you've been out of high school for a while, this is a good, reasonably priced option. These professionals help college students every day, so they have a good idea

> As you are researching your future career, mentally "try on" each job you encounter. Would you feel comfortable doing this job every day? Why or why not? Asking yourself these questions will help you focus on possibilities that not only sound interesting generally but also make sense for you personally.

of what the local job market looks like. They are also excellent sources of information about the best jobs for the future.

Private Career Counselor

You can also seek the advice of a private career counselor (sometimes called a career coach) to help you find a career. These counselors are usually employees of for-profit firms. If the initial appointment is offered for free, you can expect it to be primarily a sales pitch for paid services rather than a true counseling session, but such an appointment is a good opportunity for you to ask questions. Before you make a fee-based appointment, be sure that you know the counselor's background and experience, including his or her experience in helping those without college degrees. Ask

> The National Board for Certified Counselors is an institution that accredits career counselors. To verify the credentials of a career counselor or to find a career counselor in your area, visit www .nbcc.org/counselorfind.

for a list of people the counselor has helped and call a few of them to see what exactly he or she did. Also, make sure you know exactly how much the consultation will cost and what the counselor will do for you for that price.

Local and Federal Jobs Programs

If there is a local jobs program in your city, you can go there for help with your career search. Most of these centers are created to help those who are out of work, but often they can also help young people who are looking for career direction. Because these organizations help people move to new fields of employment, they can provide a great deal of useful information about the local job market and about careers with solid potential for the future. And like the high school guidance office and the college career center, the jobs program office will probably have databases that you can use to search for descriptions of different jobs. To find your local jobs programs, visit the website for your city or county government and look for a "Services," "Programs," or "Employment" section. For example, in Chicago, the Youth Career Development Centers, a local jobs program that offers career counseling services to young people ages 14 to 21, is listed along with other jobs programs under the section on the City of Chicago website titled "Programs and Initiatives."

Or look for your local One-Stop Career Center by entering your zip code into the location finder at www.servicelocator.org. Sponsored by the U.S. Department of Labor, One-Stop Career Centers offer such services to career and job seekers as individual career counseling appointments. The career counselor can help you define your career goals, offer you testing in skills and interest inventories, and suggest an action plan, steps to take to get you on your career path. And there is no fee for any of this help.

See What's Out There

Researching your options is an essential part of your career planning. Purchasing career books and access to career databases can be an expensive undertaking for an individual. Luckily, your local library is a treasure trove of information about careers. Talk to a librarian about your career search and ask if you can make an appointment with a reference librarian. Reference librarians are skilled at finding exactly the information you need. If you cannot find a reference librarian, you can always ask at the front desk of your local library. Any librarian can help you find the library's career information.

Be sure to ask the librarian to look for jobs and careers with the level of education you have in mind. The librarian needs to know as much as possible about your career search. If you have absolutely no idea at all, tell the librarian and ask for some ideas about where you can go to find out about careers and jobs that might interest you.

Check Out a Book or Two

There are dozens of books about determining the right career or job for you, so browsing the career section of your local library or bookstore will always turn up something. Two books to seek out specifically are *What Color Is Your Parachute?* by Richard Bolles and *If You Knew Who You Were, You Could Be Who You Are* by Gerald M. Sturman.

Although it has been years since it was first published, *What Color Is Your Parachute?* continues to have a huge impact on the job scene. Richard Bolles is a sought-after speaker on the subject of finding the right career and getting a job. Old as it is, this book is still an excellent source for finding out what you want to do with your life, and it has been updated frequently, so look for one of the newer editions. There is also a version for teens written by Carol Christen and Richard Bolles, *What Color Is Your Parachute? for Teens: Discovering Yourself, Defining Your Future.* Bolles's website, www.jobhuntersbible.com, is one of the best sources for online testing as well.

If You Knew Who You Were, You Could Be Who You Are is a career-assessment seminar all wrapped up into an easy-to-use workbook. The author, Gerald Sturman, provides a variety of career assessments in addition to career advice. This is a particularly good resource if your access to counselors and assessment tools is limited.

Use the Net

Professional career counselors or your local librarian can give you access to career databases to which they subscribe. They will also be able to direct you to Internet resources that are the most helpful and online testing tools, some of which are described later in this chapter. Most people don't think they need professional help to search the Internet, but your searches will be much faster and more productive if an expert researcher is advising you. If you want to find exactly what you want right away—without wading through hundreds of websites trying to sell you something—ask for assistance from your local librarian. There are some excellent online resources for exploring careers. Here are a few:

Exploring Career Information
www.bls.gov/k12
The U.S. Bureau of Labor Statistics, or BLS, offers a variety of excellent resources. This great job portal for high school students and graduates is one of them. The site, geared at high schoolers, lists careers by personal interest category: math, reading, science, social studies, music and arts, building and fixing things, helping people, computers, law, managing money, sports, nature, and more. Each category page provides information about specific jobs and explains how to get into these jobs, as well as how much you can make and what your day-to-day job would be like.

Occupational Outlook Handbook (OOH)
www.bls.gov/ooh
The Occupational Outlook Handbook (OOH), also published by the BLS, lists hundreds of careers along with career outlook, wages, and the education and training needed to be hired in that career.

For each occupation, the OOH provides the following information:

▶ **What they do.** What are the duties and responsibilities of people working in this occupation? What tasks do they complete on a day-to-day basis? There is a page in each occupation profile that sums up this up for you.

▶ **Work environment.** Is it dangerous work? Do people in this career work in office buildings, hospitals, homes, or outdoors? Find out by clicking on this tab in the occupation profile.

▶ **How to become one.** Some jobs you can go right into. Others require training, and still others require a certificate or degree. The OOH will let you know.

▶ **Pay.** How much would you earn? The handbook gives you an average salary for each occupation.

▶ **Job outlook.** What does the future look like for people in this profession? Will the profession be in high demand or on the decline? OOH researches and projects what each career will look like in ten years and whether it is expected to grow or not. You can find this information for every occupation in the OOH.

▶ **Similar occupations.** What other related jobs are out there? If you like the idea of being a radiologic technologist, you might love the thought of being a diagnostic medical sonographer. When you

---

Updating the BLS Occupational Outlook Handbook

The Occupational Outlook Handbook from the Bureau of Labor Statistics is revised every two years so that the information stays current. If a new occupation becomes popular or a new technology changes the way a particular job is done, the handbook is updated to reflect this. Significant changes, such as when drugstores started hiring pharmacy technicians and aides to save money and help pharmacists be more efficient, are also included in the revisions.

When you use the OOH to find information about a job you are interested in pursuing, you can be confident that it is up to date.

visit an occupation profile, you can read about related fields and occupations.

> **Contacts for more information.** Where can you learn more? Just follow the links provided in the occupation profile.

My Next Move

www.mynextmove.org

This site asks, "What do you want to do for a living?" and offers three ways to answer:

> **"I want to be a . . ."** If you know what you'd like to do for a living, you can "describe your dream career in a few words" in the blank provided, click Search, and you will be taken to a list of jobs that are relevant. Click on any of these jobs to be taken to a simple one-page summary of that job, complete with information on the knowledge, skills, and abilities you need to have to do it, along with the education and training required and even good personality traits to possess.

> **"I'll know it when I see it."** Click on a pull-down menu, select from a list of industries, and click Browse to explore occupations by the industry you want to be in.

> **"I'm not really sure."** Click Start to answer a series of questions to help guide you to information on careers you might be interested in. Based on your answers, you'll receive a list of suggested careers that match your interests and training.

One of the great features of this site is the simple and user-friendly occupation profile pages. My Next Move is sponsored by the U.S. Department of Labor.

O*NET Online

www.onetonline.org

O*NET Online is an interactive website for exploring jobs and job trends. You can search for occupations by skills, tools, and technology. To do a skills search, visit www.onetonline.org/skills.

Career Searches That Work

One of the best ways to research careers is to visit the OOH main page, www.bls.gov/ooh, and search by education. To do this, click on the button marked "Entry-Level Education" in the middle of the page, and a pull-down menu will appear. Select the level of education or training you are planning to complete, and click Go. You will get a list of occupations that will be available to you, along with the amount of on-the-job training that is required, the projected number of new jobs in those occupations in the next ten years, the occupation's projected growth rate for the next ten years, and the median pay for that occupation in 2010. Click on the name of any occupation you're interested in on the list, and you will be taken to a very detailed profile.

There are many other good ways to search for careers from the OOH main page. If you're looking for occupations that are expected to have excellent growth through 2020, click on the "Fastest Growing (Projected)" link underneath the search options, and you will get a list of the twenty jobs projected to be growing the fastest between 2010 and 2020.

You can also use the vertical navigation bar on the left-hand side of the page to browse by occupation group. If you have a rough idea of what industry or field you'd like to work in, you can pinpoint your interests by clicking on the link and viewing the occupations within that group.

Or you can browse by career cluster, industry, and keyword. An "advanced" search allows you to search for careers using the following options: abilities, interest, knowledge, skills, work activities, and tools and technology. To do an advanced search, go to the O*NET Online main page and click Advanced Search in the top navigation bar. A pull-down menu will appear, giving you these options. Any search you perform will take you to a list of relevant occupations. For example, if you search for a specific technology in a "tools and technology" search, the search results will be a list of all occupations that use that technology. Clicking on an occupation from this list will take you to a page with details about how that technology is used in that occupation. This is valuable if there is a specific technology you want to use in your career.

America's Career Infonet
www.careerinfonet.org
The main page is full of links useful for people exploring careers. Click on any of them for information and tools to help you zoom in from the big picture, but here are some of the best:

> **Occupation Information**. Clicking this link will take you to the Occupation Profile, a tool that allows you to search by keyword or select a job category. The most useful feature of this tool is that it gives detailed information for the career you're interested in.
> **State Information**. Select this link if you want a "big picture" of the careers in the state you live in or want to move to. Job outlook and salaries, among many other factors, vary from state to state. On each state profile, you can see the fastest growing occupations in that state, the average salaries for careers, and much more information, including links to free career services offered in that state.
> **Videos**. Click this box in the middle of the page to view videos about nearly 550 different occupations.

This site is sponsored by the U.S. Department of Labor, so it's free to use.

MyFuture.com
www.myfuture.com
Check out career-planning tools for young adults thinking about their next steps. This site is particularly informative about careers in military service. One tool on this website, MyPathway, will lead you through the decision-making process of finding a career and training for that career.

Consider High-Demand Careers

Look into careers that are expected to have high demand in the future. According to the Bureau of Labor Statistics, 18 of the 30 fastest-growing careers require less than a four-year degree. The following table lists the average salary earned by people in these careers and the amount of training needed for each. Several of these careers will be discussed further in

Fastest-Growing Careers Requiring
Less Than a Four-Year Degree

Occupation	Median Annual Pay (2010)	Education/Training Required
Personal and home care aides	$19,640	Short-term on-the-job training
Home health aides	$20,560	Short-term on-the-job training
Helpers—brickmasons, blockmasons, stone-masons, and tile and marble setters	$27,780	Short-term on-the-job training
Helpers—carpenters	$25,760	Short-term on-the-job training
Veterinary technologists and technicians	$29,710	Associate degree
Reinforcing iron and rebar workers	$38,430	Apprenticeship
Physical therapist assistants	$49,690	Associate degree
Helpers—pipelayers, plumbers, pipefitters, and steamfitters	$26,740	Short-term on-the-job training
Diagnostic medical sonographers	$64,380	Associate degree
Occupational therapy assistants	$51,010	Associate degree
Physical therapist aides	$23,680	Moderate-term on-the-job training
Glaziers	$36,640	Apprenticeship
Medical secretaries	$30,530	Moderate-term on-the-job training
Brickmasons and blockmasons	$46,930	Apprenticeship
Dental hygienists	$68,250	Associate degree
Bicycle repairers	$23,660	Moderate-term on-the-job training
Stonemasons	$37,180	Apprenticeship
Pile-driver operators	$47,860	Moderate-term on-the-job training

Source: Bureau of Labor Statistics Occupational Outlook Handbook, 2012–13 edition, www.bls.gov/ooh.

later chapters of this book. You can also visit www.bls.gov/ooh and search by an occupation name to see a complete profile.

Take Career and Personality Tests

If you visit a career counselor of any sort, he or she will probably have you take one or more assessment tests. These tests typically indentify aspects of your personality or define your desires for professional fulfillment and then link that information with potentially suitable careers. You may have already taken at least one of them while you were in high school. The career and personality tests offered most often are described in this section. Take as many of these kinds of tests as you can. Each one will tell you a little more about yourself and encourage you to think about what you want to do. You never know which piece of information will help you uncover your desired career path. Fees for the paid tests typically range from $10 to $100. Here are some of the most popular.

Myers-Briggs Type Indicator

The Myers-Briggs Type Indicator is a classic and widely used test that classifies test-takers into one of sixteen personality types based on four fundamental traits. The theory is that certain personality types will do well in certain career paths. For example, a person whose test results indicate he is an ESTJ (extroverted, sensing, thinking, judging) type might make a good police officer. Many colleges administer this test as part of their career counseling services for students, and companies often give this test to members of project teams to help them work together more successfully. Although you will be charged a fee to take the test, many swear that the results are particularly insightful. Visit www.mbticomplete.com to take the Myers-Briggs test online. Once you have taken the test and discovered your personality type,

Green Jobs

In 2010 the U.S. Bureau of Labor Statistics received funding to develop and implement the collection of new data on green jobs. Green jobs are generally identified as jobs that help improve the environment, save on resources, or help people use greener and more environmentally sustainable options in their lives.

To find out about green jobs, go to www.bls.gov/green/greencareers.htm.

there are many free resources on the Internet that can help you translate your results into career suggestions.

Career Key

The Career Key test works on the same principle as Myers-Briggs, linking personality traits to career characteristics, and it is used frequently to help people figure out what they will be good at. Test-takers are categorized into six career types and matched to their ideal work environment types. The idea behind this test is that people work best when they choose jobs that match their own career type and are more happy and successful when they work with people who have that same career type. To take the Career Key test online, go to www.careerkey.org and click on "Take the Career Key Test." It takes about 15 minutes to complete, and there is a small fee to take the self-assessment.

Strong Interest Inventory

The Strong Interest Inventory, one of the most popular career self-assessment tools, is designed to help people make career and educational plans. Taking it can help you find out how your interests relate to different work environments and activities and how your interests compare with individuals in a wide variety of career fields and occupations. The Strong also includes scales that measure leadership style, risk taking, team orientation, learning environment, and work style. One advantage of this assessment is that it gives you results you can benefit from if you are just starting out in your career. Your high school counselor or local community college career counselor is bound to have it, or you can purchase it online on several websites. It takes about 30 minutes to complete online and is followed by a phone or in-person consultation, which is usually included in the test fee.

O*NET Career Exploration Tools

O*NET offers a set of self-directed career exploration and assessment tools for "students who are exploring the school-to-work transition." These tools are designed to help people discover what they like to do, what is important to them in their working life, and what they do well. One of the main advantages of the tools is that users can link their results directly to occupational information in O*NET's database of more than 900 occupations to create a list of potentially compatible careers.

▸ The **Interest Profiler** is a career interest assessment instrument that promotes a user's self-knowledge about career interests, fosters career awareness, and links the user directly to a list of potential careers. You can download the software for the computerized version at www.onetcenter.org/CIP.html or complete a shortened version online at www.mynextmove.org/explore/ip.

▸ The **Work Importance Profiler** identifies work needs and values that are important to you. After you input the level of education, training, and experience you currently have or expect to have, the computer generates the Occupations Report, a list of occupations whose important work needs and values correspond with yours. Download this assessment at www.onetcenter.org/WIP.html.

Because these tools were developed by the U.S. Department of Labor, they are free to use.

Career Perfect

Career Perfect offers several good tests free of charge that help with career planning, including an interest inventory and a work preference inventory. Visit www.careerperfect.com/content/career-planning-free-tests to take them.

LiveCareer

LiveCareer offers a variety of career tests on its website, www.livecareer.com. The "Can you run your own business?" test is a good way to see if you have what it takes to start your own business. However, this site also offers interest inventories and other tests that may help if you don't know exactly what you want to do for a career. *Fair warning:* You will have to click through several screens of LiveCareer trying to interest you in educational opportunities, but the content more than makes up for the annoyance. The list of entrepreneurial skills is excellent. The reports from the interest inventories are also quite helpful. You can save and print the reports for future reference.

Conduct Informational Interviews ··

In its most basic form, an informational interview is an interview in which you ask an expert in a particular field questions. Your most important trait as an interviewer is curiosity. During an informational interview, you are acting as a reporter, gathering facts and interesting details about a person's career.

In some cases, you meet in the expert's office, but you can also invite the expert for coffee (which you will buy) to ask questions. Be respectful of your interviewee's time. Arrive early and keep the interview short (30 to 45 minutes at most).

It's a good idea to have a set list of questions to keep the interview on track, so take the time to tailor the questions to the person or occupation. No matter what you ask, be sure to get each interviewee's advice about how to choose a career. You may not agree with advice about choosing a career that pays well or choosing one that allows you to help others, but you will learn a great deal about the people you think you know and about how people choose a job or a career. More often than you would think, the job picks them.

Remember, however, an informational interview is not a job interview. Be sure to put your interviewees at ease by assuring them that you simply want to find out about their careers and are not hoping that they might have a job opening for you.

Ask People You Know

One excellent way to begin is to interview people you already know—parents, grandparents, aunts, uncles, teachers, coaches, ministers, anyone who knows you personally and has an interest in seeing you succeed—about their jobs. Keep an open mind. Even though a job may sound incredibly boring to you, you may be surprised to find that someone you know works at that job and finds it endlessly fascinating.

Ask about Jobs That Sound Interesting

If you hear about a job that sounds interesting to you, seek out a person who holds that job. Except for celebrities, most people are delighted (and even flattered) to be asked about their career path and the day-to-day workings of their job.

Sample Informational Interview Questions

How did you get into this career?

What do you like about it?

What were you hoping to do when you started in this field?

What are you still hoping to accomplish?

If you had it to do over again, would you follow the same path?

Is any formal education or training required for the job?

What are your day-to-day activities on the job?

What are your job responsibilities or duties?

What do you think are the prospects for this industry in the future?

It's even a good idea to interview one or two people with a job you think you'd never want to do. The day-to-day activities may be better than you imagine. The worst that will happen is that you learn a great deal about why that person chose that job. Observing why people do what they do is a skill that can serve you well in your professional life.

Ask Successful People

Interview someone you know who is successful at his or her career, even if that occupation doesn't sound like it's for you. Anyone who has found success in a career will likely have valuable insights that are generally applicable to any career. If you don't know anyone who is as success-ful as you want to be, ask a librarian for help in identifying community leaders.

Look Back at Yourself

Don't forget this: What you would like to do for a job is directly related to what you like to do. Period. Filling out the Career Interest Inventory at the end of this chapter is a way to help you figure out what you wanted to be as you grew up. Remembering what you wanted to be back then may just help you figure out what you want to be now. For example, knowing that you liked math back in grade school may cause you to ask yourself if you still like math. If you do, there are many jobs that require math skills.

The same goes for science, English, and many other subjects. If you can remember what you used to like to do, it can help you ask a variety of good questions to help you figure out what you like to do today. And what you like to do today can help you choose a career.

If you've decided that a four-year college degree is not for you, you may think that your career options are limited. But you couldn't be more wrong.

There are many good jobs out there, but the best jobs do require some kind of additional training after high school. To make it easier to find exactly what you want in this book, I divide job opportunities into four categories, which we will cover in the next four chapters: jobs without formal training (chapter 2), jobs with formal training (chapter 3), jobs that require a certificate (chapter 4), and jobs that require a two-year degree (chapter 5).

Career Interest Inventory

	Choice 1	Choice 2	Choice 3
Elementary School			
Favorite subjects			
Favorite teachers			
What you wanted to grow up to do or be			
What you did after school			
Heroes or role models			
Favorite books			
Favorite relatives			
Middle School/Junior High School			
Favorite subjects			
Favorite teachers			
What you wanted to grow up to do or be			
What you did after school			
Extracurricular activities or clubs			
Heroes or role models			
Church activities			
Volunteer activities			
Favorite books			
Favorite relatives			

(cont.)

Career Interest Inventory (cont.)

	Choice 1	Choice 2	Choice 3
High School			
Favorite subjects			
Favorite teachers			
Extracurricular activities			
Clubs or organizations			
Sports			
Church activities			
Volunteer activities			
Heroes or role models			
Favorite books			
Favorite relatives			

TWO

Jobs without Formal Training

Learning on the Job

Many people are sick of school after high school and want to go right into the work world. They may decide to go back to school later, or they may be so successful in their career choice that they don't need the extra education. You don't need a college education to be successful, as Steve Jobs, the founder of Apple Computer, made clear in his own life. However, not everyone is a certifiable genius. Just because there are no formal educational requirements for certain jobs doesn't mean that you won't be learning something.

Jobs without formal training are positions in which you will still train on the job. Some companies may have an internal training program. Other companies may give you a mentor to help you learn the job. Still others allow you to learn on your own. The good news is that you are often paid for your training time.

Although you may not earn a piece of paper to show what you've learned, most companies expect their workers to keep learning throughout their time at the job. New technological tools are developed almost every day, and you will be expected to learn to use the company's business tools as they are updated.

This chapter deals specifically with jobs that you can get without a degree, certificate, or apprenticeship. We look at a variety of jobs that pay while you learn and the kinds of personalities and skills that are required to get them. From the previous chapter, you already know how to search for additional jobs and job information online and at your local library. If the jobs listed here don't interest you, you have all the tools to find some that do.

Another route into the work world without formal training is starting your own business. You can be sure that you'll learn on the job if you take this path. That's where we begin this chapter.

Owning Your Own Business

According to the U.S. Small Business Administration (SBA), "each year, more than 10 million people consider starting a business. Of them, only three million people take the plunge and start a business. It's one of the most exciting endeavors that any person can undertake."

Although owning your own business doesn't require formal training, you will be learning a great deal every single day as a business owner. If you are already the type of person who has mowed lawns, done babysitting, or run errands for others, you may have exactly the right entrepreneurial personality to start your own business.

Starting a Business

If you want to start your own small business, a Small Business Development Center (SBDC) in your area should be one of your first stops. To find the SBDC closest to you, visit the national Association for Small Business Development Centers website, www.asbdc-us.org, and enter your zip code or state in the location finder. Or use the interactive map to find your regional SBDC website. The great thing about an SBDC is that you can take its online business classes for free and get one-on-one training and advice about starting a business. Assistance from an SBDC is available to anyone who cannot afford the services of a private consultant and is interested in beginning a small business for the first time or wants to improve or expand an existing small business.

The SBDC can give you information about starting or running a small business, including getting loans or grants for your small business, marketing your business, and writing a business plan. One SBDC article suggests twenty questions that you should ask yourself before you start your own business:

- Am I prepared to spend the time, money, and resources needed to get my business started?
- What kind of business do I want?
- What products/services will my business provide?
- Why am I starting a business?
- What is my target market?
- Who is my competition?
- What is unique about my business idea and the products/services I will provide?
- How long will it take before my products/services are available?
- How much money do I need to get my business set up?
- How long will I have to finance the company before I start making a profit?
- Will I need to get a loan?
- How will I price my product compared to my competition?
- How will I market my business?
- How will I set up the legal structure of my business?
- How will I manage my business?
- Where will I house my business?
- How many employees will I need to start up?
- What types of suppliers do I need to contact?
- What kind of insurance do I need to invest in?
- What do I need to do to ensure I am paying my taxes correctly?

You can also read a helpful article on the SBA website that outlines the ten steps you need to take to start your own business at www.sba.gov/content/follow-these-steps-starting-business.

It's possible you may want to work with another family member in the family business. This is also an excellent option that does not require formal training. But you will probably want to take a class or two in areas where you may not have a natural talent, such as accounting, marketing, or human resources. To decide whether you might need a class or two, take a couple of the SBA's free online courses (register at www.sba.gov/content/online-courses-starting-your-business), particularly Technology 101: A Small Business Guide and How to Prepare a Business Plan. If your business needs require more training than what is presented in these classes, try taking a couple of formal classes. See chapter 6 for information about where to look for reasonably priced, convenient classes.

Do You Have the Entrepreneurial Spirit?

Many people think they can't start their own business unless they go to business school. According to the Small Business Administration, anyone can learn how to be an entrepreneur. The SBA notes that entrepreneurs often have common traits and characteristics and lists some that can go a long way toward bolstering business success:

Creative

Inquisitive

Driven

Goal-oriented

Independent

Confident

Calculated risk taker

Committed

Avid learner

Self-starter

Hard worker

Resilient (able to grow from failure or change)

High energy level

Integrity

Problem-solving skills

Strong management and organizational skills

Don't worry if you don't have all these traits to start with, note the experts at SBA. Most traits can be learned with practice.

Buying a Franchise

If you don't have a family business to run and you don't know what kind of business you would like to run, you can buy a franchise such as a fast-food restaurant or gas station. The company that sells you the franchise will train you to run the company, and franchise businesses are often quite lucrative.

The Small Business Administration offers a free half-hour online course that walks you through the basics of franchise ownership. The course is self-paced, so you can stop and start as often as you like. Register for the class by visiting the SBA's online course list at www .sba.gov/content/online-courses-starting-your-business and clicking on Franchising Basics.

Sales Jobs

One good job option that doesn't usually require formal training is sales. Every company in the world needs people to sell its products to consumers or to other companies. If you are outgoing, well-spoken, and you like to deal with people, this could be the job for you. The pay can also be excellent if you are good at what you do.

Here are two facts about sales jobs from the Bureau of Labor Statistics (BLS):

▸ Earnings usually are based on a combination of salary and commission.
▸ Employment opportunities and earnings may fluctuate from year to year because sales are affected by changing economic conditions.

Job titles range widely, from sales representative to advertising sales agent, and there are sales jobs in almost every industry. However, most sales positions share certain characteristics. For example, the job of a salesperson is to cause customers to be interested in the goods or services being sold and to sell those goods or services to the customer. In addition, the sales cycle can take a great deal of time, depending on the product.

Salespeople talk on the telephone to potential customers; show customers their products one-on-one during demonstrations, trade shows, or sales calls; explain the benefits of their goods or services; and answer customer questions. Some salespeople sell to consumers; others sell to the government or to other companies. All salespeople need to keep up with the latest products and technologies in their field.

Salespeople can work inside an office or be on the road traveling most of the time. Some can determine their own hours; others need to spend a certain number of hours inside an office or showroom. The job can be stressful because the income is often based on commission. In addition, some companies promote salespeople within the organization on the basis of how much they sell, so it can be quite competitive. Most organizations set sales goals or quotas for their sales force.

Although there is usually no formal education required for sales jobs, many salespeople attend seminars, conferences, and webinars to help them keep up with new products and sell more effectively. Some companies have in-house training programs for their sales force, and others pair a sales trainee with a seasoned salesperson for training purposes.

Selling Yourself

Grace Prumella grew up being crazy about anything with an engine. She followed NASCAR every weekend on television and even studied each racing team online. For a while, Grace considered becoming an automotive mechanic, but later she decided that she could put her knowledge of cars to another use.

After high school, she applied for a sales job at a local car dealership. The sales manager treated her application as a joke at first. Instead of getting mad or giving up, Grace gave the sales manager her most charming smile and bet him that she could sell a car to the next customer who walked in the door. If she didn't make the sale, she said, she would never bother the sales manager again.

Grace never doubted that she would get the job. "I knew everything about every car on the lot," Grace explains. "When a mom came in with two kids in a stroller, I asked her about her family and her future plans. We were just two women talking. Then I showed her a high-end station wagon instead of the minivans that all of her friends were driving. That was probably the easiest sale I'll ever make. The sales manager's jaw just hung open in surprise. I think I'm really going to like my new job. In five years, I plan to have that sales manager's job."

According to the BLS, the employment of sales representatives is expected to grow in the next ten years, about as fast as the average for all occupations. If you have good communication skills, persistence, and self-confidence, you might be very well suited to being a sales professional.

Careers in the Arts

If you like to draw, take photos, sing, or play an instrument, you might decide to be an artist. Some artists go on to get a degree in their area of art, but you don't necessarily have to. Be warned, though: it can be difficult to make a living as an artist. And to be a professional artist, you will need discipline, talent, perseverance, and physical stamina.

Visual Arts

Before you decide that it's an artist's life for you, you may want to do a BLS search on this career. The BLS lists several important points to consider before you decide to pursue art as a job:

- Almost 60 percent of visual artists and related workers are self-employed, so you will most likely have to pay for benefits such as health insurance yourself.
- Keen competition is expected for both salaried jobs and free-lance work because the arts attract many talented people with creative ability.
- Artists usually develop their skills through a bachelor's degree program or other postsecondary training in art or design in order to enter such careers as graphic designer, multimedia developer, animator, or art director.
- Earnings for self-employed artists vary widely; some well-established artists earn more than salaried artists, while others find it difficult to rely solely on income earned from selling art.

To research the various types of possible jobs for artists, visit the BLS's Exploring Career Information profile on artists and musicians, www.bls.gov/k12/music.htm.

Performing Arts

If you dream of performing in front of an audience, this may be the career for you. However, you need to keep in mind a few points from the BLS:

▸ Many musicians, dancers, and singers have part-time work schedules—typically at night and on weekends. In addition, intermittent unemployment and rejection when auditioning for work are common. Many performers supplement their income with earnings from other sources.

▸ Aspiring musicians, dancers, and singers usually begin studying an instrument, taking dance lessons, or training their voice at an early age.

▸ Competition for jobs, especially full-time jobs, is fierce; talented individuals who can play several instruments and perform a wide range of musical styles should enjoy the best job prospects.

Many musicians learn to play several related instruments and can perform equally well in several musical styles. Instrumental musicians, for example, may perform in a symphony orchestra, rock group, or jazz combo one night, appear in another ensemble the next, and play in a studio band the following day. Some play a variety of string, brass, woodwind, or percussion instruments or electronic synthesizers.

Singers use their knowledge of voice production, melody, and harmony to interpret music and text. They sing character parts or perform in their own individual styles. Singers often are classified according to their voice range—soprano, contralto, tenor, baritone, or bass—or by the type of music they sing, such as rock, pop, folk, opera, rap, or country. Singers perform in bands, sing for live audiences, or record in studios.

About 40 percent of dancers work in performing arts companies, and nearly 80 percent of choreographers, who

---

Need More Job Options? Ask a Librarian

If you want to know about more jobs that provide on-the-job training and pay you while you learn the job, go to your local library and ask a librarian. Librarians can point you to books, databases, and online resources for jobs with good pay that train you while you work.

create original dances and develop new interpretations of existing dances, work in schools, including dance and fine arts schools. Dancers and choreographers in dance companies travel for months at a time. And injuries take a toll on the body: dancers have one of the highest rates of nonfatal on-the-job injury. Most dancers stop performing in their thirties, and many become choreographers, directors, or dance teachers.

Singers, dancers, and musicians can supplement their income by giving private lessons, but in order to teach in a school environment, they will likely need to have a bachelor's degree.

If you want to know more about careers in the performing arts, go to www.bls.gov/k12/music.htm.

Jobs with On-the-Job Training

The Bureau of Labor Statistics divides jobs without formal training into three categories: jobs with short-term on-the-job training, jobs with moderate-term on-the-job training, and jobs with long-term on-the-job training. In this section, we review several jobs from each category, so you can see what types of jobs you can get with each level of get-paid-as-you-go training.

Jobs with Short-Term On-the-Job Training

The sample jobs chosen for this section either have a relatively high wage or are in great demand (as rated by the BLS). Sample jobs in this category are postal service mail carriers; cargo and freight agents; meter readers for utility companies; and secretaries and administrative assistants.

Postal Service Mail Carriers
If you have customer-service skills, stamina, physical strength, and a good driving record, you might make a good postal service mail carrier. Qualification for this job is based on an examination. But before you sign up to take the Postal Service examination, think about the following points from the BLS:

> ▹ The number of jobs is projected to decrease by about 12 percent over the 2010–2020 period due, in part, to new automated sorting systems and the downturn in the economy.

▸ Very strong competition for available jobs is expected.
▸ Applicants usually remain on a waiting list for one or two years after passing the Postal Service examination and before being hired.

As you probably know, mail carriers for the Postal Service deliver mail to people's houses and businesses in your neighborhood and around the country. What you may not know is that postal carriers come in early to sort the mail. In addition, they may walk their route or drive it, depending on the city where they work. Mail carriers often carry a heavy pack full of mail, and they can work long hours. They also have to work during the hottest days of summer and the coldest days of winter. Remember, mail carriers spend most of their time outdoors, so this is a job for people who prefer not to work in an office.

According to the BLS, since this job category is supposed to decrease, there will be keen competition for the jobs that remain. This job will fare better than other Postal Service jobs, however: clerk positions are projected to decline by 48 percent, and mail sorters by 49 percent, by 2020.

For more information, visit the Postal Service's career page, at http://about.usps.com/careers.

Cargo and Freight Agents

Cargo and freight agents have good record-keeping, customer-service, and computer skills and are very organized. If you think that describes you, read on. Cargo and freight agents are in charge of overseeing incoming and outgoing shipments for many different kinds of companies. Here are some important facts about this occupation from the BLS:

▸ Employment is expected to grow by an impressive 29 percent through 2020, so the job outlook is good.
▸ Cargo and freight agents have a higher-than-average rate of injury and illness; injuries are usually minor and include pulled muscles, cuts, and bruises.

Cargo and freight agents supervise the movement of shipments of goods through shipping docks and airline, train, and truck terminals. They are responsible for ensuring timely pickup and delivery of shipments, filling out any necessary paperwork, and collecting fees. International shipments can require a complex set of documents and are governed by very strict rules. Cargo and freight agents fill out customs and tariff forms and make sure everything is in order. Often, the job requires working out of warehouses that are not temperature controlled or outside on a loading dock. Agents may need to carry small items around, but they use forklifts to move heavy cargo. You can view a short but informative video from America's Career InfoNet that gives a good overview of the career at www.careerinfonet.org/videos.

Meter Readers

If you have good time-management, math, and customer-service skills and dislike the thought of sitting in an office all day, you might thrive as a meter reader. The bad news is that meter readers, people who go around reading water, gas, and electric meters at homes and businesses, are shrinking in numbers, according to the BLS.

> ▸ Most meter readers work for electric, gas, or water utilities.
> ▸ New technology allows meters to be monitored remotely, reducing the need for meter readers. Most utilities have not implemented this technology yet, so there are still job opportunities out there.

The good news is that there are still job opportunities because of the need to replace people who are leaving this occupation. Also, some new automated meter reading systems work from a car or truck. This requires fewer meter readers, but it still uses them in the field. For a short video from America's Career InfoNet, visit www.careerinfonet.org/videos.

Secretaries and Administrative Assistants

If you are computer literate, a "people" person, are organized, and have good writing skills, you might be interested in becoming a secretary or administrative assistant. Most secretaries and administrative assistants work in comfortable office settings, where they perform routine clerical and organizational tasks, such as organizing files, drafting correspondence, scheduling appointments, and supporting other staff.

> ▸ The BLS expects this occupation to grow by 12 percent through 2020.

Outlook for Jobs Requiring Short-Term On-the-Job Training, 2010-2020

Jobs for which short-term on-the-job training is the most significant source of postsecondary education or training.

Occupation	Employment (in thousands)		Employment Change		Jobs Growth/ Replacement 2010–2020 (in thousands)	2010 Median Annual Wages
	2010	2020	No. (in thousands)	%		
Postal Service mail carriers	316.7	278.5	-38.1	-12.0	103.4	$53,860
Cargo and freight agents	82.2	106.3	24.1	29.3	44.2	$37,150
Meter readers	40.5	41.0	0.5	1.2	12.7	$34,820
Secretaries and administrative assistants, except legal, medical, and executive	2,032.2	2,150.8	118.5	5.8	391.0	$30,830

Source: Bureau of Labor Statistics Selected Occupational Projections Data, http://data.bls.gov/oep.

> Many temporary agencies provide training in computer and other necessary skills, and a temporary assignment can be a foot in the door to a full-time position.

Secretaries and administrative assistants work in almost every kind of organization, including schools, government agencies, and private corporations. Secretaries are often responsible for handling much of the communication in an office, and some of this information is confidential, such as student or medical records, salary and budget information, or personnel documents. Good secretaries and administrative assistants have to be discreet and professional.

There are some excellent advancement opportunities in this occupation. Many secretaries and administrative assistants move up to become executive secretaries (who made an average of $43,520 in 2010), clerical supervisors, or office managers.

For more information on becoming a secretary or administrative assistant, visit www.bls.gov/ooh/office-and-administrative-support/secretaries-and-administrative-assistants.htm.

Jobs with Moderate-Term On-the-Job Training

The jobs in this section usually rely on moderate-term on-the-job training and are considered by the BLS to have a relatively high wage or to be in great demand. Sample jobs in this category are correctional officers and jailers; dispatchers for police, firefighters, and ambulances; pharmacy technicians; and court, municipal, and license clerks.

Correctional Officers and Jailers

Correctional officers keep the peace in state and federal prisons, local and county jails, and other detention facilities. The good news about this occupation is that the wage is relatively high. The bad news is that this job can be dangerous and stressful. But if you have the critical-thinking skills, good judgment, physical strength, and self-discipline to handle yourself in this kind of environment, you might be a good fit. Before you apply to be a correctional officer, consider these facts from the BLS:

> Correctional officers have one of the highest rates of nonfatal on-the-job injury.

Outlook for Jobs Requiring Moderate-Term On-the-Job Training, 2010–2020

Jobs for which moderate-term on-the-job training is the most significant source of postsecondary education or training.

Occupation	Employment (in thousands)		Employment Change		Jobs Growth/ Replacement 2010–2020 (in thousands)	2010 Median Annual Wages
	2010	2020	No. (in thousands)	%		
Correctional officers and jailers	475.3	499.8	24.5	5.2	108.1	$39,040
Dispatchers for police, firefighters, and ambulances	100.1	111.8	11.7	11.7	30.7	$35,370
Pharmacy technicians	334.4	442.6	108.3	32.4	166.3	$28,400
Court, municipal, and license clerks	129.5	139.9	10.4	8.0	46.7	$34,390

Source: Bureau of Labor Statistics Selected Occupational Projections Data, http://data.bls.gov/oep.

▹ Officers must be physically fit and often have to meet certain physical requirements.

Officers process new prisoners, watch video surveillance of prisoners, search prisoner cells or the prisoners themselves, and enforce institution rules. They may also process prisoners out of the facility or escort prisoners out of the facility as needed for court dates.

The BLS notes that prisons are safer work environments than jails because the population is more stable. Jail populations change frequently and can be difficult to predict.

Since jails and prisons need to be protected 24/7, corrections officers can work at any hour or on any shift. They can also work on holidays and weekends.

Although corrections officers learn most of their job on the job, they also attend training academies. In addition, some facilities prefer candidates with previous law enforcement experience, military service, or college courses.

Job prospects are favorable for this career through 2020. Prisons in rural areas seem to have more difficulty finding appropriate candidates. If you are interested in this career, you may have a better chance finding your first job if you look in rural areas with a prison nearby.

For more information, visit www.bls.gov/oco/ocos156.htm.

Dispatchers for Police, Firefighters, and Ambulances

Dispatchers, also referred to as 911 operators, take emergency calls and send emergency services workers to the proper location. Dispatchers must be able to keep a cool head in an emergency situation and be able to multitask. They should have excellent listening, problem-solving, and leadership skills.

▹ The projected growth rate for this occupation is 12 percent, about average with all other occupations.
▹ Dispatchers often have to work nights, weekends, and holidays because emergency services are available 24/7.

The typical education required for an entry-level position is completion of high school or a GED. However, some states, counties, and cities may require a specific certificate or training for their dispatchers. Applicants for a dispatcher position must have an interview, as well as pass a written exam and a typing test. They may also have to take hearing and vision tests and pass a drug screening.

Training for this job varies by state, and some states require 40 or more hours for new dispatchers. The good news is that this training is usually done on the job, so you will be paid for it.

Dispatchers usually work in a call center.

The BLS expects this job to have good prospects for the future and for employment to hold steady through 2020. Those with excellent computer skills or the ability to speak a second language should have the best opportunity for employment. Experienced dispatchers can get promoted to senior dispatcher or supervisor, with a bump in pay and responsibility.

For more information, see www.bls.gov/oco/ocos343.htm.

Pharmacy Technicians

If you have good customer-service and organizational skills and are detail oriented, you might be the ideal candidate for this fast-growing occupation. Pharmacy technicians help dispense prescription medication. The BLS offers a few points to consider:

▷ Due, in part, to more medications being used to fight disease, the projected growth rate for this occupation is an impressive 32 percent.
▷ Pharmacy techs usually work in a comfortable, indoor environment, but they are on their feet for many hours a day.

Pharmacy technicians help pharmacists prepare prescriptions for patients and keep track of prescriptions according to state and federal laws. Techs may count pills, receive requests from patients, label bottles, and handle administrative duties. The responsibilities vary by position and location. In a large retail pharmacy, a pharmacy tech may work more closely with registered pharmacists to dispense prescriptions. In a smaller pharmacy, he or she may deal with patients and other pharmacy customers more frequently. Most pharmacy technicians work in pharmacies located in grocery stores, hospitals, drugstores, mail-order companies, and warehouse facilities.

Pharmacy techs may have to work evenings, nights, weekends, and holidays, depending on where they work. They also handle confidential medical information and must be discreet and professional.

There is no national standard for pharmacy techs. Some have certificates, and others learn on the job. A few states license them. If you are good with numbers and have never had a drug conviction, you could be a pharmacy tech.

The outlook for this occupation is favorable. As the U.S. population ages, more pharmacy techs will be needed to help pharmacists keep up with the demand for prescription medications.

For more information and to learn the requirements for this profession in your state, visit the website for the National Pharmacy Technician Association at www.pharmacytechnician.org.

Court Clerks

Court clerks keep the records of the court for which they work. If you are organized, a good communicator, and have computer skills, you might consider this occupation.

▷ According to the BLS, this occupation is growing due to more demand for government and court services.
▷ Because they work for city or county governments, court clerks often have excellent benefits and attractive pay.

Clerks of the court perform a variety of clerical duties for government licensing agencies and bureaus. They can also work for municipalities or in courts of law. They can prepare the calendar of cases, also known as the docket, for the court or prepare bylaws for a town council. They may also keep records and accounts for their office or bureau. Some even collect fees.

A high school diploma is generally enough for most positions, but some employers prefer hiring clerks with additional education. Most are trained on the job in the policies and procedures of the government agency that employs them.

For more information, see www.bls.gov/ooh/office-and-administrative -support/information-clerks.htm.

Jobs with Long-Term On-the-Job Training

The jobs in this section have long-term on-the-job training and are listed by the BLS as having relatively high median annual wages or are projected to be in demand in the next decade. Sample jobs in this category include purchasing agents; claims adjusters, appraisers, examiners, and investigators; water and wastewater treatment plant and system operators; and dispensing opticians.

Purchasing Agents

Purchasing agents do exactly what you would think. They buy goods and services for their companies or organizations. This job requires solid analytical and decision-making skills, as well as a good grasp of math. It also doesn't hurt to be a good negotiator. The BLS notes the following about this occupation:

> ▹ Employment is expected to grow by about 5 percent through 2020, a bit below the average for all other occupations.
> ▹ To advance in this career, agents often need to continue their education while on the job. Additional education or advanced certificates are suggested for those who want to rise to management positions.

Purchasing agents seek the best possible price for everything their company uses. They also have to be aware of sales forecasts and the best suppliers, and they must know something about each product they intend to buy. Some buyers purchase goods for consumer companies such as department stores and online retailers. Others buy goods for their corporation, such as paper, office supplies, computers, and copiers.

Purchasers usually work in offices and may put in more than 40 hours in a week. They often interview new companies to find out if they would be good suppliers. They also attend conventions or trade shows to learn about the latest trends in their industry. Some buyers travel extensively for their companies in order to find new suppliers or interesting new products.

In most cases, people in this profession start out as junior buyers, clerks, or assistants. Some companies prefer to hire applicants with a two-year or four-year college degree; it depends on the company. Training can last as long as five years or as short as two years. Each company has its own training program. In many instances, the training period depends on the complexity of the company's business or the products it buys.

For more information, see www.bls.gov/oco/ocos023.htm.

Outlook for Jobs Requiring Long-Term On-the-Job Training, 2010–2020

Jobs for which long-term on-the-job training is the most significant source of postsecondary education or training.

Occupation	Employment (in thousands) 2010	Employment (in thousands) 2020	Employment Change No. (in thousands)	Employment Change %	Jobs Growth/ Replacement 2010–2020 (in thousands)	2010 Median Annual Wages
Purchasing agents (except wholesale, retail, and farm products)	284.2	299.3	15.1	5.3	91.2	$56,580
Claims adjusters, appraisers, examiners, and investigators	280.1	288.4	8.3	3.0	79.9	$58,620
Water and wastewater treatment plant and system operators	110.7	123.6	12.9	11.6	41.5	$40,770
Dispensing opticians	62.6	80.7	18.1	28.9	30.6	$32,940

Source: Bureau of Labor Statistics Selected Occupational Projections Data, http://data.bls.gov/oep.

Claims Adjusters, Appraisers, Examiners, and Investigators

Most people buy one or more types of insurance. In fact, car insurance is required by law in all but a few states. If you are in a car accident, you will submit a claim to your insurance company. Claims adjusters, appraisers, examiners, and investigators process those claims. They also investigate insurance claims, negotiate settlements, and make arrangements for checks to be mailed out. To do one of these jobs, you need to have analytical, communication, and interpersonal skills, as well as a good grasp of math. The BLS provides the following facts about this career.

 ▹ Employment is expected to grow by 3 percent by 2020, a bit below the average for all other occupations.
 ▹ Insurance investigators often work odd schedules in order to conduct surveillance and interview people not available during normal business hours.

These four jobs tend to overlap. Specific tasks vary depending on the company. People in these jobs could go out to view the damage of a hurricane, for example, and take pictures. They could also process claims in the office. Or they might look over claims that have been processed to be sure that all the company's rules have been followed.

Appraisers are generally people who look at items and determine what they are worth. Investigators, as the name implies, go out and investigate claims that the insurance company thinks may be fraudulent.

So far there is no specific training for this occupation. Each insurance company has its own rules. Some insurance companies seek only those with a two-year or four-year college degree; others hire people with a high school diploma. In most cases, adjusters, examiners, appraisers, and investigators are hired at a junior level and work with an experienced person on the job to learn what is required. As each person improves, he or she is given more responsibility. Most of these jobs require attending seminars, conferences, and continuing education to stay current on claim fraud and other insurance issues. Some states require that those in these jobs be licensed.

The BLS expects these job opportunities to be best in the health insurance industry and in regions susceptible to natural disasters.

For more information, see www.bls.gov/oco/ocos125.htm.

Water and Wastewater Treatment Plant and System Operators

Water treatment plant and system operators manage technology that pumps fresh water from natural sources into water treatment plants, where it is treated. They make the water safe to drink and then send it out to customers.

Wastewater treatment plant and system operators perform a similar operation, but they remove pollution from home and industrial wastewater. Wastewater flows through sewage pipes to wastewater treatment plants, where the operators treat it and return it to natural water sources.

Consider these important facts from the BLS:

▸ Employment is expected to grow by 12 percent through 2020, about as fast as the average for all other occupations.

▸ Workers in these occupations must pay close attention to safety procedures because of hazardous conditions, such as slippery walkways, dangerous gases, and malfunctioning equipment. As a result, workers experience an occupational injury and illness rate that is much higher than the average for all occupations.

Plant and system operators run the machines that cleanse and purify water. They can monitor gauges in the plant, test water for impurities, or manage other workers. System operators can work inside and outside. They can repair machinery or monitor computer screens.

According to the BLS, employees in this occupation usually start out in junior positions as operators-in-training or attendants. They learn on the job by working with seasoned veterans who show them how to record readings, take samples, and maintain the equipment.

Plant and system operators need a high school diploma and are usually skilled at fixing things and knowledgeable about basic math, chemistry, and biology. Some employers prefer to hire applicants with a certificate or an associate degree in water quality management or wastewater treatment technology.

This occupation is licensed by the states. Most states have four levels of licenses, and each increase in license level allows the operator to control a larger plant and more complicated processes. At large plants, plant and system operators who have the highest license work as supervisors and may be in charge of other operators.

For more information, visit the Work for Water website, www.workforwater.org.

Dispensing Opticians

Opticians help fit eyeglasses and contact lenses according to prescriptions written by ophthalmologists and optometrists. They also help customers choose eyeglass frames and contact lenses. Since they work so closely with customers, they need to have good communication and customer-service skills. Since they often repair or make fine adjustments to eyeglasses, they need to have good manual dexterity.

▶ This occupation has a high growth rate (29 percent), due, in part, to an aging population in need of corrective lenses.
▶ Opticians who work in large department stores may be required to work evenings and weekends.

Some opticians work in stores that sell glasses and contact lenses. These may be stand-alone stores or part of a large department store. Other opticians work in optometry or ophthalmology practices.

Opticians usually learn their job through formal on-the-job training programs. However, twenty-three states now require licensing. An optician becomes licensed through a formal training program or apprenticeship.

For more information on this growing occupation, visit the American Board of Opticianry and National Contact Lens Examiner website, www .abo-ncle.org. For help locating a training program or apprenticeship for this occupation, turn to chapter 6 in this book.

If you feel like formal training is something you'd like to explore, continue on to the next chapter. There are some great opportunities available for people who are open to completing additional training.

THREE

Jobs with Formal Training

Where Apprenticeships and Specialized Training Can Take You

To get some jobs, you'll need to go through a formal training program. The good news is that with many of these jobs, the training programs are free, and you are paid while you train.

For some careers, like carpenter or plumber, people often train through apprenticeship programs that offer classroom instruction and real-world experience. For others, such as careers in the armed forces, you are trained in the military's own specialized training program. Some careers, such as police officer and firefighter, have their own academies but may require real-world experience, physical fitness, and some education beyond high school. Some companies will even send the people they hire, including those with a high school diploma, to a formal training program or training school or set them up in an apprenticeship program.

Although you may not graduate from these programs with a sheepskin or a piece of paper, you will learn a skill that can earn you a living.

The jobs detailed in this chapter are only a few examples of the many jobs out there for someone who is willing to receive extra training after high school. From chapter 1, you already know how to search for additional jobs and job information through the Bureau of Labor Statistics and your local library. If the jobs listed here don't interest you, you have the knowledge you need to find other jobs that do.

Jobs with Their Own Training Programs ···················

Some jobs are so specialized that they have their own training programs and academies. You might find that doing the extra training is worth it for some of these jobs. Plus, for these jobs, the employer often takes care of all your training, so there are generally no costs to you, such as tuition, fees, or supplies. The specialized nature of these training programs means you really nail down the essentials of the job, and you don't have to learn a lot of things you won't need to do your job effectively.

> You can get an excellent job by completing a formal training program. Many apprenticeship programs offer both classroom instruction and real on-the-job training that you're paid for. In addition, these jobs are frequently associated with a union, so they generally have good wages and benefits.

The Armed Forces

Going into the U.S. military is an option for many people. Each branch has its own training facilities. You get paid while you are in training, and your pay increases as you gain experience and more training. The military also provides you with housing, meals, and health insurance. Most branches administer an entrance examination to determine what you are good at. The bad news is that you often don't get to choose where you are posted.

The BLS notes the following facts about military careers:

▸ Even in peacetime, duty assignments and training can be dangerous.
▸ Military personnel must obey strict rules of military conduct both on and off duty.
▸ People who serve for twenty years in the military are eligible for retirement and receive a military pension.

Those who enlist in the armed forces serve in the Army, Navy, Marines, Air Force, or reserve units. They do the actual work of the military: building schools, working in hospitals, writing up requisitions for supplies, and the thousand other tasks required both in peacetime and in war. The major occupational groups within the armed forces include the following:

- Administrative workers
- Combat specialists
- Construction workers
- Electronic and electrical equipment repairers
- Engineering, science, and technical personnel
- Health care personnel
- Human resources development specialists
- Machine operator and production personnel
- Media and public affairs personnel
- Protective service personnel
- Support service personnel
- Transportation and material-handling specialists
- Vehicle and machinery mechanics

The work environment depends on the branch of the service, posting, and job designation. Many in the armed forces spend months or years away from their families.

Those who serve in the military sign a contract and agree to serve for a specific amount of time. They can reenlist multiple times if they like. Recruits are given a variety of tests to determine their skills. They are also sent to a specific basic training location based on their job classification, their branch of service, and their unit. While in the service, you can get more training and go to a variety of training schools or bases all around the world. However, your commanding officer usually determines what additional training you will get.

The main placement test used in the armed forces is the Armed Services Vocational Aptitude Battery (ASVAB). Based on your scores, you will have a variety of choices about your branch of service and training. Much of this information can be included in the enlistment contract. To get into the military, you also have to pass a physical exam.

Enlisted personnel have to go through basic training, also called boot camp. This training may last six weeks or longer

> ### Need More Job Options?
> ### Ask a Librarian
>
> If you want to know about more jobs with formal training, go to your local library and ask a librarian. The librarian can point you to books, databases, and online resources for jobs with good pay that offer their own formal training.

Outlook for Jobs Requiring Formal Training, 2010–2020

Jobs for which formal training is the most significant source of postsecondary education or training.

Occupation	Employment (in thousands)		Employment Change		Jobs Growth/ Replacement 2010–2020 (in thousands)	2010 Median Annual Wages
	2010	2020	No. (in thousands)	%		
Firefighters	310.4	336.9	26.6	8.6	112.3	$45,250
Police and sheriff's patrol officers	663.9	718.5	54.6	8.2	249.4	$53,540
Plumbers, pipefitters, and steamfitters	419.9	527.5	107.6	25.6	228.8	$46,660
Carpenters	1,001.7	1,197.6	196.0	19.6	408.3	$39,530
Brickmasons and blockmasons	89.2	125.3	36.1	40.5	54.5	$46,930
Stonemasons	15.6	21.4	5.7	36.5	8.9	$37,180
Chefs and head cooks	100.6	99.8	-0.8	-0.8	18.0	$40,630

Source: Bureau of Labor Statistics Selected Occupational Projections Data, http://data.bls.gov/oep.

and includes strenuous physical activity and military training. After basic training, enlisted people are usually sent for additional technical training in their job specialty. In many instances, recruits can receive college credit for their military training. In addition, recruits can also qualify for tuition credits from the military and additional training after their enlistment is over.

The U.S. military is required to help its personnel transition back into the civilian work world, and it works with certifying associations to make sure members of the armed forces receive formal recognition in the private sector for their technical training. Many enlisted personnel are eligible to receive civilian certifications in such occupations as air traffic controller, dental assistant, and more.

Even in the twenty-first century, women are mostly excluded from direct exposure to combat. Women do, however, become mechanics, medical personnel, and fighter pilots as well as holding positions in a variety of other specialties.

In 2011, more than 2.3 million people served in the armed forces, and more than 1.4 million of them were on active duty. The BLS expects that 165,000 recruits will be needed each year to replace retirees and those who will complete their enlistment requirements.

There are nine pay grades for enlisted personnel; visit www.bls.gov/ooh/military/military-careers.htm to see these salaries and to read more about careers in the military.

Firefighters

Being a firefighter is a difficult but rewarding job. And, depending on where you live, it can be hard to find a job with your local fire department. In the past few years, the career of firefighter has changed a great deal. It went from being an on-the-job training career to one that now looks for candidates with a background in fire science. However, depending on where you live, you can still find fire departments that do their own on-the-job training.

▶ Employment is expected to grow by about 9 percent through 2020.
▶ Firefighters have a higher rate of injury and illness than the national average.

▷ Because the majority of calls firefighters are sent on are medical, not fire, emergencies, most fire departments prefer to hire applicants with an emergency medical technician (EMT) certification.

Everyone knows that firefighters put out fires. However, they are also called to be first responders in many other situations, including traffic accidents and other emergencies. When fighting fires, they work as a team, and they may also provide emergency medical treatment. Some firefighters are also specially trained to deal with hazardous materials or forest fires.

Firefighters often work long hours and can work nights, weekends, and holidays. They usually start their shift at the fire station. Then, when an alarm sounds, they are off to fight a fire or deal with another emergency. Some firefighters work 24 hours on and 48 hours off. Others work daytime hours with occasional overnight shifts.

Firefighters must be in good physical shape because the gear they wear is heavy, and they are often required to run up and down ladders while fighting a fire. This work is highly dangerous and can be stressful as well.

Individuals applying to be firefighters are usually given written tests as well as physical ones. Most firehouses put applicants through a real-world test to see if they can carry all the gear, run up a ladder, and get in and out of a burning house.

After being hired, rookie firefighters attend a local training academy or center to learn about fighting fires. They are taught in the classroom and in practice training. Some fire stations also have accredited apprenticeship programs that give rookies formal and on-the-job training under the supervision of experienced firefighters.

The BLS expects employment for firefighters to grow slightly slower than average through 2020. There will be a great deal of competition for the positions that are available, for this is a popular occupation. In rural areas it may be harder for fire stations to find qualified firefighters; in larger cities, fire stations may find more qualified candidates. Taking one or more classes in fire science at the local community college may help you get a job in your local fire station. An EMT certification also helps; in some fire departments, you can earn this certification after you are hired.

There is opportunity for advancement to positions such as engineer, lieutenant, and battalion chief. First-line supervisors of firefighting and prevention workers with up to five years of work experience earned a median wage of $68,240 in 2010.

For information on how to find classes in fire science and EMT certification training programs, see chapter 6. For information on how you can get an edge on being hired as a firefighter, visit the website FireRecruit.com and click on Articles in the left-hand navigation bar. This section has great advice on what to do if you are interested in joining this profession.

Police and Sheriff's Patrol Officers

If you have always wanted to "serve and protect" and you have good communication and leadership skills, the ability to connect with others, as well as good judgment, strength, and stamina, you might be cut out to be a police officer. The BLS notes the following facts about working as a police or sheriff's patrol officer:

- The work can be stressful and dangerous; police officers have one of the highest rates of on-the-job injury and fatality.
- Bilingual applicants have the best job prospects.
- Those with experience in the military police or some college classes in police science are expected to be preferred over other candidates.

Police and sheriff's patrol officers protect people and their property. They write tickets, apprehend criminals, and prepare a wide variety of

Earning a Badge

Jilly Enbrooke dreamed of going into the family business. Her father, grandfather, and uncle had all been police officers. Her grandfather had even been police commissioner.

Jilly joined the track team in high school to keep herself in peak physical condition, so she could ace the physical training component of the police academy. She is planning to continue her education in the future, but she wants to attend the police academy first. She's been accepted into the next academy class.

"I've always wanted to help people," she says. "I can't think of a better way to contribute to the community or the world than by being a police officer. It's all I ever dreamed of as a kid."

reports. Police officers must maintain excellent records because they are often asked to testify in court.

Police may work at a wide variety of levels of government. Some work for a specific city; others, sheriffs and deputy sheriffs, work for a particular county. State police officers work for a specific state; they are often highway patrol officers or state troopers. This career can be dangerous and stressful. In addition, long hours can make it difficult to have a personal life. Although officers are supposed to work a regular 40-hour week, most police stations pay a great deal of overtime. Officers may also work nights, weekends, and holidays.

To apply to be a police officer, candidates need only a high school diploma. Much of the training of a police officer is done on the job after academy training. Candidates need to be at least twenty-one and physically fit. Candidates younger than twenty-one can begin as cadets, who perform clerical duties and attend classes until they have reached the minimum age requirement. The following elements are usually part of any hiring process:

- Background check
- Written exam
- Physical fitness test
- Drug and alcohol test

Being bilingual or having one or more college courses in law enforcement can help you move to the top of the candidate list.

A rookie police officer is usually hired at a police department and then sent to that department's police academy for training. It costs nothing for the officer trainees to attend the academy, and they also receive their salary while training. Less commonly, you can also pay to attend a police academy before being hired by a department. In this case, you'll have to pay your own tuition expenses, and some police departments will reimburse a portion of that tuition when they hire you. Police academies require anywhere from 320 to 800 course hours and usually last six to eight months, depending on the state's requirement. Recruits receive classes in constitutional and state law, writing reports, firearms, strategic driving, crime-related procedures, car crash investigation, traffic law, arrest techniques, and physical fitness, among other topics.

After several years on the force, police officers may advance to detectives, who are responsible for investigating crimes and collecting evidence. The median salary for detectives in 2010 was $68,820.

The occupation is growing a little more slowly than the national average, according to the BLS. The population growth in cities is causing the most growth in law enforcement careers. Some jobs will also be added because of retirements in the police force or officers joining federal law enforcement.

For a good overview on what kind of training you'll receive in a police academy, visit "How Police Academies Work" on HowStuffWorks at http://people.howstuffworks.com/police-academy1.htm. For tips on finding classes in criminal justice, see chapter 6. For more information about what police officers do, visit the BLS profile at www.bls.gov/ooh/protective-service/police-and-detectives.htm.

Apprenticeships: Get Paid to Learn a Trade

Getting an apprenticeship in a local trade union is another option for people who don't want to go to a four-year college. You apply to be accepted and then you get on-the-job training from a fully licensed professional. This type of job can pay very well, but it can also be difficult to get into the "trades" (which generally means occupations that involve some mechanical skills) unless you know someone who's already in them. Having a friend or family member in the trades can be very helpful in getting you accepted into an apprenticeship program.

Plumbers, Pipefitters, and Steamfitters

This employment classification generally has five specialties:

- Plumbers install and repair items in your home that involve water, waste drainage, or gas systems. They may also work in commercial buildings or in industry.
- Pipelayers lay pipes for sewers, drains, water mains, or gas or oil lines.
- Pipefitters work with low-pressure and high-pressure pipes that carry chemicals, acids, and gases.
- Steamfitters install systems that move liquids or gases under high pressure.
- Sprinklefitters install and repair the sprinkler systems in buildings.

Plumbers usually work inside homes and businesses, but the other specialists may work outside or in industrial locations. Workers in this trade need to be strong enough to lift and carry heavy pipes. They must also be able to get into small or cramped locations to reach pipes. Some may be on call at night and on weekends and holidays in case of emergencies.

Most people in these professions start with a union apprenticeship program, but some complete apprenticeship programs through community colleges or technical schools. Apprenticeship programs consist of four or five years of paid on-the-job training, including up to 2,000 hours of training and a minimum of 246 hours of technical classroom instruction for each year. Some states also require plumbers to be licensed.

The BLS projects that this profession will grow by 26 percent by 2020, which is much faster than average, with very good job opportunities.

For information on how to find an apprenticeship program or trade union, see "How Do I Find an Apprenticeship?" in chapter 6. For more information about this occupation, visit the Careers section of the United Association (the union of plumbers, pipefitters, welders, steamfitters, sprinkle fitters, and HVAC service techs) website at www.ua.org/careers .asp.

Carpenters

Carpenters build structures, usually from wood. They are involved with building everything from kitchen cabinets to bridges. Some carpenters specialize in a specific area, but most can perform a wide variety of jobs. There can be a high degree of creativity and artistry involved in this profession, depending on the complexity of the project. If you are detail oriented and have a good grasp of basic math, manual dexterity, and physical strength, you might be interested in this trade.

> ‣ Employment is expected to grow by 20 percent through 2020.
> ‣ Carpenters experience a higher than average rate of injury and illness, the most common being muscle strains and cuts from sharp tools and other objects.

The BLS estimates that more than a third of carpenters are self-employed, and most work in the construction industry. Some carpentry projects are difficult and strenuous. Carpenters may also work outside or in harsh environments and may need to kneel, stand, or bend for long periods of time, depending on the job.

Many people start carpentry careers by being accepted into an apprenticeship program through a union, technical school, or community college. The apprenticeship can take up to four years and involves learning about structural design and common carpentry tasks on the job by working with more experienced carpenters and taking classes. People who cannot get into apprenticeship programs can take college courses at a technical school or community college. Sometimes this type of training can help you get a job with a construction company. Because they learn the entire construction process, carpenters are more likely to be promoted to supervisory positions or to become independent contractors.

For details on how to find an apprenticeship program in carpentry, see "How Do I Find an Apprenticeship?" in chapter 6. For more information on being a carpenter, visit the Occupational Outlook Handbook profile at www.bls.gov/ooh/construction-and-extraction/carpenters.htm.

Brickmasons, Blockmasons, and Stonemasons

Like carpentry, masonry work requires a high degree of creativity. If you're a creative person, with physical stamina, dexterity, strength, and math skills, you might be suited to being a mason. The BLS notes:

> ▹ This is a quickly growing career, with employment projected to grow by as much as 41 percent (for brickmasons and blockmasons) and 37 percent (for stonemasons) by 2020.
> ▹ Masonry work has a much higher rate of injury and illness than the national average; muscle strains are the most common.

Brickmasons and blockmasons, also called bricklayers, build and repair walls and other structures made of brick and masonry panels, such as fireplaces, chimneys, and outdoor grill, patio, and walkway areas. Stonemasons build stone walls and set stone exteriors and floors with natural-cut stone, such as marble or granite, and artificial stone made from concrete and other materials. They use a special hammer or a diamond-blade saw to cut stone into specific shapes and sizes.

Both stonemasons and bricklayers read blueprints, estimate the amounts of building materials needed for a project, lay out brick or stone patterns, and ensure that the structure built is square and level and built to specification.

About a third of masons are self-employed. Most masons work on houses, but masonry work on nonresidential buildings is becoming more common. Masons do a lot of their work outdoors and, at times, in dangerous locations, such as from a scaffold on the side of a building.

Some masons learn on the job, and some complete masonry programs at a technical college. But to become a mason, you will most likely have to enter an apprenticeship, usually lasting three to four years and requiring at least 144 hours of technical instruction and 2,000 hours of on-the-job training each year. You may have to start as a construction helper. After their apprenticeship is complete, masons are considered *journey workers* and are able to work on their own. Credits earned as part of an apprenticeship program often count toward an associate degree.

For details on how to find an apprenticeship program in masonry or a local masonry trade union, see "How Do I Find an Apprenticeship?" in chapter 6. For more information on being a mason, visit the website for the Mason Contractors Association of America, www.masoncontractors .org.

Chefs and Head Cooks

Even if you can only cook one or two simple dishes, you can learn to be a chef or head cook. Many people start training for this profession with nothing but a passion for food and a desire to work in the restaurant business. If you have the desire; creativity, leadership, time-management, and business skills; and a good sense of taste and smell, you can become a chef or head cook. The BLS notes the following:

▶ There is a 1 percent decline in employment projected for this occupation, which means there will be little or no change in demand for chefs and head cooks. However, there will be a good number of job openings due to the need to replace workers who leave the occupation or retire.

▶ The job can be stressful and chaotic, as chefs and head cooks work in hectic environments and stand on their feet for long periods.

Chefs and head cooks manage kitchens and plan meals and inventory for restaurants and any other place where food is served, such as college dormitories or cruise ships. They may create their own recipes, hire and train kitchen staff, and select and purchase ingredients. Here are some of the most common jobs in this field:

▹ Executive chefs plan menus and oversee the operations of a kitchen, usually at a large restaurant or bar.
▹ Sous chefs are next-in-command to the head chef. They supervise the cooks and may be in charge of ingredient preparation.
▹ Personal chefs cook for people in their own homes. They are usually in charge of stocking groceries, planning meals, and cooking. They may also serve meals and wash dishes and can work for a service that provides cooking for homes.

Most people in this profession start off as line cooks or even dishwashers, learning as they go. More and more, people are attending community colleges or culinary academies to learn to cook. Some chef training programs take four years, but most take only two. You apply to them as you would to any college, and they often have a screening test to see if you have the right aptitude for the job. Most training programs require some kind of internship or apprenticeship.

You can also enter into an apprenticeship program without taking classes first. Formal apprenticeship programs often last two years and involve both work experience and classes. The American Culinary Federation, trade unions, and culinary institutes sponsor many of these.

Once you're accepted into the program, it's all about learning how to cook for a crowd. Most programs teach you how to cook for large facilities such as restaurants, resorts, and hotels. You may also learn how to run a restaurant and how to organize a professional kitchen.

For information on finding a community college or culinary arts school that is right for you, visit the website for the American Culinary Federation, www.acfchefs.org, and select Education in the navigation bar at the top. You will see a drop-down menu of choices, which include Postsecondary Programs, Apprenticeships, and Scholarships. Select any of these to get more information. See also the sections on finding apprenticeships and certificate programs in chapter 6.

If you need help filling out job, apprenticeship, or school applications, see chapters 7, 8, and 9. They give you advice on how to put your best foot forward and get the position you're applying for or a spot in the training program you're interested in. If you'd like to explore the jobs you can get with a certification, turn to the next chapter.

FOUR

Jobs with a Certificate

Where Credentials Can Take You

If you are interested in gaining some credentials but don't want to invest four more years in school, a certificate program may be right for you. You can get a variety of good jobs by completing a certificate program at a community college or vocational school. Certificates usually take from one to four semesters to earn depending on your area of study, and many can be completed in a year or less.

The beauty of the certificate is that it proves that you have been trained to do something. Another benefit is that many institutions that grant certificates also have excellent job placement services for those who earn

---

What Is a Certificate?

You can spend from just a few months to a couple of years earning a certificate. A certificate can give you the education and credentials to apply for several relatively high-paying jobs. You just need to find a certificate program that interests you.

Certificate programs are offered by community colleges, vocational schools, for-profit educational institutions, and even online. To find a certificate program in the occupation you're interested in, see "Where Will I Earn My Certificate?" in chapter 6. There are several websites that can help you find the right program after you've decided what you want to be.

---

certificates. So, you can spend a short time earning the certificate and looking for your first job.

In this chapter we look at a variety of jobs that require a certificate. You already know how to search for additional jobs and job information through the BLS and your local library. If the jobs listed here don't interest you, you learned in chapter 1 how to find some that do.

HVAC Mechanics and Installers

HVAC (heating, ventilation, and air conditioning) technicians work with the total air quality system in industrial, residential, and commercial facilities. They usually install the equipment, repair it, or maintain it. Some HVAC technicians specialize in installation or repair; others can do both. Virtually every building in the nation has an HVAC system that needs maintenance or repair.

If you have mechanical skills, dexterity, and strength, you might want to consider this fast-growing occupation. A talent for troubleshooting is also a definite plus.

> ▸ The BLS projects that this occupation will grow by an impressive 34 percent through 2020, much faster than average. Many businesses are upgrading to more energy-efficient climate-control systems. Demand for this occupation is growing so quickly that many contractors are having a hard time finding HVAC technicians.
> ▸ HVAC technicians often have to work in hot or cold environments to repair broken climate-control systems.

HVAC technicians work in commercial buildings, warehouses, homes, hospitals, and factories. They may work inside one day and outside another. Technicians must squeeze into HVAC spaces, which are often small and cramped, and they may also be required to work in attics and ceiling spaces.

Although HVAC technicians usually work a regular 40-hour week, they may be required to work extra hours during peak seasons. Some will also be on call in case of emergencies. The BLS notes that, as HVAC systems evolve, technicians will also need to know more about computers, which are increasingly used to monitor commercial, industrial, and residential HVAC systems.

HVAC technicians usually receive formal training and earn a certificate at a technical school or community college. The certificate program can take from six months to two years to complete. It is possible to receive several levels of certification from such various accrediting organizations by taking competency exams. For information about these certifications, visit the following websites:

▶ Air-Conditioning, Heating, and Refrigeration Institute, www.ahrinet.org
▶ HVAC Excellence, www.hvacexcellence.org
▶ National Occupational Competency Testing Institute, www.nocti.org

Some HVAC technicians are trained in the military. Some training is also offered in apprenticeship programs, which normally last three to five years. Some states and regions require HVAC techs to be licensed. Some technicians may also need to be certified to work with refrigerants.

To find a certification program, visit the aforementioned websites or turn to chapter 6 and read the section on finding certificate programs. You can also find information on apprenticeships for this occupation in chapter 6.

For more information on this occupation, see www.bls.gov/oco/ocos192.htm.

Seeking a Certificate? Ask a Librarian

Your local library and the librarians who work there are some of the most efficient and cost-effective resources in your community. If you are interested in earning a certificate in order to get a better job, your local library is a great place to get started. Ask the research librarian on staff to help you search for certificate programs that interest you, or ask for help finding out what you are interested in doing for a career.

Whatever you need to know, your local library has the information, including DVDs, CDs, websites, books, and databases. Go in and find out for yourself how helpful the library can be.

Outlook for Jobs Requiring Certificate Training, 2010–2020

Jobs for which certificate training is the most significant source of postsecondary education or training.

Occupation	Employment (in thousands)		Employment Change		Jobs Growth/ Replacement 2010–2020 (in thousands)	2010 Median Annual Wages
	2010	2020	No. (in thousands)	%		
HVAC mechanics and installers	267.8	358.1	90.3	33.7	137.6	$42,530
Surgical technologists	93.6	111.3	17.7	18.9	33.9	$39,920
Court reporters	22.0	25.1	3.1	14.1	6.4	$47,700
Sound engineering technicians	19.0	19.1	0.1	0.6	5.5	$47,080
Licensed practical and licensed vocational nurses	752.3	920.8	168.5	22.4	369.2	$40,380

Source: Bureau of Labor Statistics Selected Occupational Projections Data, http://data.bls.gov/oep.

Surgical Technologists

Did you know that you can perform a vital role in an operating room without earning a four-year degree? Surgical technologists, also called operating room technicians, scrubs, or surgical techs, assist in surgeries by prepping patients, arranging equipment, and being in charge of surgical tools. During an operation, they are the members of the surgical team who pass tools to the surgeons.

Consider these facts about this occupation from the BLS:

> ▸ Job opportunities are expected to grow faster than average, by about 19 percent by 2020.
> ▸ Currently hospitals hire the most surgical technologists, but employment is expected to grow in other health care settings.

Surgical technologists also dispose of or preserve specimens, such as biopsies or tumors that have been removed from the patient. They stand for long periods during an operation and must be able to deal with the sight of blood and other unpleasant sights and odors that are common in an operating room. Surgical technologists need to have a strong stomach, as well as good manual dexterity, stamina, and stress-management skills. Attention to detail is crucial. Most surgical technologists work a regular 40-hour week, but they may be on call at certain times in case of emergency surgeries.

Surgical technologists can get a job with a certificate, which can be earned within a few months to two years. Certificate programs are offered by hospitals, community colleges, and technical schools. Some surgical techs can earn a certificate with on-the-job training in the military. Others may also have earned an associate degree from a community college. Some specialize in particular types of surgery, such as transplants.

One good thing about certification is that it can help a surgical tech get a job. Certain certifications allow the use of the title "Certified Surgical Technologist" or "Tech in Surgery—Certified."

For information on accredited training programs, visit the website for the Commission on Accreditation of Allied Health Education Programs, www.caahep.org, or turn to chapter 6 and read the section on how to find certificate programs.

For more information on surgical technologists, download the brochure *Creating the Optimal Surgical Environment: Today's CST and CSFA* from the website for the Association of Surgical Technologists: www.ast.org/professionals/documents/BROCHURE-ASTCSTCSFA.pdf.

Court Reporters

Many people are surprised to learn that court reporters don't just work in courts of law. Some also work at public events to create word-for-word transcriptions and captioning, and others provide captioning for television programs. If you have excellent concentration and listening and writing skills, you might consider becoming a court reporter.

▶ This occupation is expected to grow by 14 percent through 2020, due, in part, to new federal legislation requiring Internet broadcasts to be captioned for the hearing-impaired in much the same way television broadcasts are.

▶ Employment in this profession could be negatively affected by the use of digital audio recording technology (DART). Some court reporters are being replaced by this new technology. However, there are questions about the accuracy of DART, so most employers still prefer to hire professional court reporters.

There are four types of court reporters, mainly distinguished by the type of equipment each uses:

▶ Stenographers use *stenotype machines* to record dialogue. Stenotype machines look like keyboards but record words and phrases through various key combinations the stenographer has learned, allowing him or her to keep up with the pace of conversation. Typing each word letter-for-letter would simply take too long, and much would be missed.

▶ Some court reporters use a *steno mask*, an odd-looking device that covers the reporter's mouth. Steno masks muffle the sound of the court reporter speaking into it so court proceedings are not disturbed. The court reporter repeats what is being said, identifies the speaker, and reports any significant physical gesture of the speaker, and the machine records it. The recording is converted by a computer into a transcript through voice-recognition software.

▷ Other court reporters use digital recording equipment to record proceedings directly and take notes to identify the speakers and narrate what is going on. They may then create a transcript by listening to the audio recording and their own notes.

▷ Court reporters who work with the deaf and hearing impaired provide *communication access real-time translation (CART)* for their clients. This involves providing live captioning for people who are, for example, visiting their doctor or taking a class and need to understand what is being said. This can be done over the Internet, in person on a small screen or tablet, or on a large screen behind the speaker, if it is a public event.

Court reporters can suffer from repetitive stress injuries resulting from hours at a keyboard. They usually work a regular 40-hour week but may work additional hours if needed. Some court reporters are self-employed and have flexible work schedules.

The training and education required for this job depend on the specialty. Programs for court reporters who use steno masks usually take six months, and a certificate is earned when the program is completed. Stenotype court reporters need more training than electronic reporters and transcribers. Their training programs often last two to four years, and sometimes the trainee will earn an associate degree. In addition to their training on different pieces of transcription equipment, court reporters also need to be able to deal with the stress of deadline pressures and time constraints. Licensing of this occupation differs by state.

For information on certifications for court reporters and broadcast captioners, visit the website for the National Court Reporters Association, www.ncra.org, or turn to chapter 6 and read the section on certificate programs.

For more information on this career, see www.bls.gov/oco/ocos152 .htm.

Sound Engineering Technicians

If you've ever run sound for your friend's band or you're the one everyone asks to set up a new home theater or entertainment system, you might thrive as a sound engineering technician. A knack for understanding the components of sound amplification, recording, and mixing is important but not the only talent you'll need. Successful sound engineering techs have excellent communication, technical, and computer skills and manual dexterity. They also solve problems creatively.

The BLS notes several significant facts about this career, including the following:

> ▸ The pay in cities is higher for this occupation, so job seekers in metropolitan areas will face more competition for the best positions.
> ▸ Sound engineering technicians can work at radio and television stations, businesses, and schools and in the recording, motion picture, and video industries.

Sound engineering technicians use sophisticated digital equipment to record, amplify, mix, or synthesize voices, sound effects, soundtracks, music, and any kind of sound. Their skills can be used to amplify a presentation at a school or conference, mix the soundtrack for a movie or other video production, amplify and provide sound effects for theater productions or musical performances, record albums or audiobooks, or any other event or purpose in which sound is an important component.

Technicians in this field may work in a comfortable studio environment or out in the field at many different kinds of indoor and outdoor events. Some sound engineering technicians have to lift and carry heavy equipment. Deadlines are often an important part of this job, which can be stressful.

Overall, employment is expected to grow only about 1 percent through 2020. However, many schools and businesses are building cutting-edge facilities to use for virtual meetings and conferences, online education, long-distance job interviewing, and live presentations. The increasing use of this kind of technology will not only help with employment growth for sound engineering technicians, but will also make certain kinds of travel increasingly unnecessary, which is good for the environment and for many companies' budgets.

Although sound engineering technicians can enter the profession with a high school diploma, it is much better to receive technical training from a community college or technical school. Sound engineering techs often complete a program and earn an audio engineering certificate. These programs only take up to a year to complete, and they will give you an edge in what is a very competitive field. A certificate lets a potential employer know that the sound engineering tech knows industry standards and provides an advantage over other job applicants. To find out more about certificate programs for this occupation, visit the website for the Society of Broadcast Engineers, www.sbe.org, or see "Where Will I Earn My Certificate?" in chapter 6 of this book.

For more information on this career, see www.bls.gov/oco/ocos109 .htm.

Licensed Practical and Licensed Vocational Nurses

You've probably heard of registered nurses (RNs), but did you know there's a nursing occupation that only requires a certificate? Licensed practical and professional nurses (LPNs), also called licensed vocational nurses (LVNs), provide basic nursing care under the supervision of RNs and doctors.

> ▶ According to the BLS, employment is projected to grow by 22 percent through 2020, which is faster than the average for all other occupations. As the U.S. population gets older and as many procedures that used to be done in hospitals are now being done on an outpatient basis in other facilities, there is more demand for nursing care in a variety of settings. A significant number of LPNs are expected to retire in the next few years, so job prospects for those wishing to enter this field are good.
>
> ▶ Nursing is demanding work: LPNs and LVNs often work nights, weekends, and holidays. Nursing shifts may sometimes last longer than eight hours.

LPNs and LVNs monitor patients in nursing care and extended care facilities, hospitals, doctors' offices, and patients' homes by taking vitals and performing other testing and evaluations. They change bandages, insert catheters, and help patients bathe and perform daily tasks while under care, such as eating and dressing. They're responsible for keeping records on the patient and keeping nurses and doctors informed about how the patient is doing.

The tasks LPNs and LVNs can perform are highly regulated and vary from state to state. LPNs and LVNs with some years of experience can supervise other LPNs and LVNs and other staff, such as orderlies.

Important qualities to have if you want to enter this profession are compassion, attention to detail, interpersonal skills, the ability to express yourself well, and physical and emotional stamina. LPNs and LVNs deal with many potentially depressing or disturbing situations, and a healthy mindset about illness and death helps nurses cope with this kind of stress. They also occasionally need to help lift or support a patient, so most nurses are fairly strong.

There are opportunities for advancement in this profession: LVNs and LPNs can be promoted to supervisors. If you are a licensed nurse and like what you are doing, you can enter an LPN to RN education program and become a registered nurse. Registered nurses earned a median wage of $64,690 in 2010.

LVNs must go through an accredited program, usually lasting one year, which can be completed at technical schools and community colleges. You will earn a certificate when you graduate from the program. Contact your state board of nursing for a list of accredited programs; to find your state board of nursing, visit the National Council of State Boards of Nursing website, www.ncsbn.org. For more information about licensed nurses, visit the National Federation of Licensed Practical Nurses website, www.nflpn.org.

Some certificate programs take close to two years to complete. There is another two-year option, the associate degree, which is the topic of the next chapter. If some of the jobs you can get with an associate degree appeal to you, you might want to consider this option.

FIVE

Jobs with an Associate Degree

Where Two Years of College Can Take You

If you're open to taking classes for a couple more years after high school, you can earn an associate degree. With only four semesters of college, you can qualify for a wide variety of careers and earn good money to start. You can attend a two-year technical, vocational, or community college (sometimes referred to as a junior college), earn an associate degree, and get a job in the field you have chosen.

In this chapter, we look at some jobs projected to be in high demand in the next few years and some others that the Bureau of Labor Statistics lists as having relatively high wages. You already know how to search for additional jobs and job information through the BLS and your local library. If the jobs listed here don't interest you, you have all the tools from the earlier chapters to find some that do.

Funeral Service Managers, Directors, Morticians, and Undertakers

You probably didn't grow up thinking, "I want to be a funeral director when I grow up," but you may be surprised by what a good job it is. And the pay is excellent.

Some important facts about this job from the BLS:

▷ Employment is projected to grow by almost 20 percent by 2020, and many funeral directors are expected to retire or leave the profession. Job prospects should be favorable, particularly for those who also embalm.

▷ Although handling bodies for burial or cremation may seem hazardous, the health risk associated with this profession is minimal. Funeral directors follow strict health and safety regulations.

Funeral directors, also called morticians or undertakers, work with the families of people who have died to set up wakes, memorial services, burials, and funerals. They put notices in local papers, work with various cemeteries for burial, and arrange logistics with florists. They also make sure that the funeral and burial go according to the deceased's wishes and the wishes of the deceased's family. It is also the duty of the funeral director to prepare the body and the burial arrangements in compliance with the deceased's religion.

Funeral directors are usually also embalmers. Embalmers wash the body and replace the blood with embalming fluid, which preserves the body until the funeral. Embalmers may also use makeup and other tools and supplies to make the body look more natural.

Funeral directors normally work in a funeral home, which has viewing rooms, caskets, and an area for embalming. They must deal with the

A Career with Job Security

"My friends don't understand why I'm studying to be a funeral director," explains Allyce Raines. "But when my mother died the people at the funeral home were so nice to me. They explained everything clearly to my dad and made the whole process of choosing a casket very easy. He just looked in a catalog. They had a showroom of caskets, but they knew it was going to be too hard for him to go in there."

Allyce has a summer job at a local funeral home and already has a wardrobe of three suits. "I like helping people," she says. "There is no better way to help people than when they are grieving for loved ones. I want to do that for a living."

paperwork associated with death, including death certificates. The hours can be long because funeral directors may have to pick up bodies at all hours.

Important personal qualities for this career are the ability to empathize with those who have lost loved ones, and interpersonal and time-management skills. Those who work in funeral homes need to maintain an appropriate appearance, which usually means short hair for men and suits for both men and women.

Funeral directors are licensed in all states, but the laws vary. Most of them require applicants to be at least twenty-one years old, have a two-year associate degree in mortuary science, serve an apprenticeship, and pass a test; others do not require an apprenticeship. In addition, funeral directors in some states may be required to take continuing education classes each year as they work in their profession.

If you are interested in this profession, you might consider seeking an internship or summer job at a local funeral home to see the job on a day-to-day basis.

> **Need More Job Options? Ask a Librarian**
>
> If you want to know about more jobs that require a two-year degree, go to your local library and ask a librarian. The librarian can point you to books, databases, and online resources for jobs with good pay that require only four semesters of college.

Those who embalm and who are willing to relocate will have the best job opportunities. For information about finding an associate degree program or apprenticeship program in mortuary science, see chapter 6 or visit the website for the American Board of Funeral Science Education, www.abfse.org.

Paralegals and Legal Assistants

If you write and express yourself well and are interested in law, you might have what it takes to work in the legal field. Paralegals and legal assistants conduct legal research, maintain legal files, and draft documents. The BLS gives the following facts about this occupation:

- ▶ Paralegals who work for law firms often work long hours.
- ▶ Paralegals can specialize in trial law, personal injury, corporate law, intellectual property, bankruptcy, family law, and many other areas.

Paralegals, also called legal assistants, work with lawyers to prepare legal documents, including looking up case law, preparing reports, researching and analyzing information, and keeping track of computer databases and exhibits for trials. In some legal offices, paralegals may also draft contracts, assist with tax return preparation, and coordinate other employees at the firm. Most paralegals work in law firms, but they can also work in corporate or government offices.

In states where paralegals are licensed, most are required to have a two-year degree. In general, paralegals with a two-year degree get paid more than those with on-the-job training or just a certificate. However, their level of experience also plays a role in their salary.

Depending on where they work, paralegals spend most of their time in law libraries or legal offices. Some may also travel to find information needed for a case. Some paralegals work a regular 40-hour week, but those who work with trial teams in law firms may work long hours before and during a trial. Those who work for tax attorneys may also work long hours during tax season.

The most common way to become a paralegal is to study at a community college for two years and earn an associate degree in paralegal studies. Some law firms even train paralegals on the job. One way to improve your chances of getting hired is to be certified by a national paralegal organization. For example, the National Association of Legal Assistants/Paralegals (NALA) offers certification for paralegals, as do other national organizations for this profession. Some states require ongoing continuing education for paralegals.

Jobs for paralegals are expected to grow about as fast as the average for all other occupations, by 18 percent through 2020. In addition, law firms are hiring more paralegals to do tasks that used to be done by attorneys. For more information about paralegals, visit the website for the National Federation of Paralegal Associations, www.paralegals.org. For information on finding an associate degree or certificate program, see chapter 6 or visit NALA's website, www.nala.org.

Respiratory Therapists

What could be more important than helping someone breathe? If you want to work in a growing health field, are patient and compassionate, and have good interpersonal, science, and math skills, consider becoming a respiratory therapist. Note these facts from the BLS:

▶ Employment is projected to grow by 28 percent through 2020, much faster than the average for all other occupations. This is due, in part, to a growing elderly population, who are more susceptible to many lung diseases.

▶ Respiratory therapists stand on their feet for many hours and may need to have the strength to be able to turn and adjust patients.

Working under the direction of a doctor, respiratory therapists work with patients who have cardiopulmonary disorders or breathing problems. They work with doctors and other health care practitioners to provide therapies and modify care plans for patients. People in this profession may perform diagnostic tests, interview patients, and do physical examinations as well as perform a variety of therapeutic treatments required for patients with breathing difficulties.

Depending on where they work, respiratory therapists can work part-time or a regular 40-hour week. In hospitals, respiratory therapists can work any schedule because hospitals are open 24/7. Some respiratory therapists work with in-home patients. Those in this profession spend a great deal of time walking to see patients and standing. The profession can also be stressful. Respiratory therapists may also work with patients who have communicable diseases and must take strict precautions.

According to the BLS, a two-year associate degree is the minimum educational requirement to become a respiratory therapist. However, to advance in this profession you should consider earning a bachelor's or master's degree. In most states, respiratory therapists must be licensed.

For more information about respiratory therapists, visit the website for the American Association for Respiratory Care, www.aarc.org. For information on finding a respiratory therapy associate degree program, see chapter 6.

Occupational Therapist Assistants

Occupational therapist assistant is one of the fastest-growing jobs in the United States. If you're interested in helping people who are recovering from injuries and disabilities develop and improve the skills they need to get back to living as independently as they can, your job prospects are promising. Good qualities to have for this job include compassion, patience, interpersonal skills, and discipline. It also helps to have a certain amount of physical strength, as you will be assisting people who may only be able to stand or move with your physical support.

Here are some facts from the BLS:

  ▸ Employment is expected to grow by 41 percent through 2020, a
    rate much faster than the average for all other occupations. This is
    due, in part, to an aging population but also to the fact that occupa-
    tional therapists are using more assistants in hospitals and in other
    settings, such as rehabilitation centers and in patients' homes.
  ▸ Only 15 percent of occupational therapist assistants worked
    in hospitals in 2010; others worked in offices of physical,
    occupational, and speech therapists; nursing care centers;
    elementary and secondary schools; and homes (for home health
    care services).

Occupational therapist assistants work with occupational therapists to
improve the quality of life for patients and help them do daily activities
more easily and even get back out into the working world. Often this
involves specialized equipment that the occupational therapist can tailor
to the patient's needs. The occupational therapist assistant will then teach
the patient how to use and maintain the equipment. Occupational therapist
assistants may also provide therapeutic activities for children with devel-
opmental disabilities. Assistants may handle paperwork, such as preparing
reports on a patient's progress or billing the patient's health insurance.

People in this profession may also work all hours of the day or on
weekends. Those who work in doctors' offices are more likely to work
more regular schedules than those who work in hospitals or with in-home
patients.

Assistants to occupational therapists are required to have a two-year
associate degree from an accredited program; most states also license
them. To advance in this career, assistants may need to complete additional training or a bachelor's degree.

For more information about this profession, visit the profile on
ExploreHealthCareers.org at http://explorehealthcareers.org/career/7/
occupational_thereapy_assistant. For help finding an associate degree
program, see chapter 6 or view the full list of accredited programs at the
website for the Accreditation Council for Occupational Therapy Education at www.aota.org.

Dental Hygienists

The person at the dentist's office who cleans your teeth is a dental hygienist. Dental hygienists also examine patients for gum and tooth disease,

take X-rays, keep treatment records, and teach patients good oral hygiene. Here are some facts from the BLS about this profession:

> ▶ This is one of the fastest-growing occupations through 2020, with 38 percent growth in employment projected. As the U.S. population ages and people are beginning to understand the important relationship between oral health and overall health, there is more demand for dental care.
> ▶ Flexible scheduling is a common feature of being a dental hygienist. Most dental hygienists work part-time; many work for more than one dentist.

Dental hygienists work with patients in a dentist's office. They teach patients good brushing skills and remove deposits from their teeth. Depending on the state where they work, hygienists may be allowed to do additional tasks often done by a dentist.

Dental hygienists wear protective gear, as all dental employees do. They may also work nights and weekends, depending on the dentist's office. Dental hygienists work closely with dentists and other dental office employees to track the progress of each patient.

This job requires licensing by the state. Some dental hygienist programs grant an associate degree, but others grant a certificate. In private practices, it is most common for a dental hygienist to have an associate degree in dental hygiene.

To find a community college with a program that's right for you, see "Where Will I Earn My Associate Degree?" in chapter 6. If you'd rather take the certificate route, see "Where Will I Earn My Certificate?" in the same chapter.

You can also visit the website for the American Dental Hygienists' Association, www.adha.org.

Diagnostic Medical Sonographers

The imaging equipment used by diagnostic medical sonographers is right on the cutting edge of medicine, and it offers patients a noninvasive and safe way to be tested for many different diseases, disorders, and injuries. Since you will be working closely with patients, to be a medical sonographer, you must have excellent interpersonal skills and a good degree of discretion and compassion.

Here are some important facts from the BLS:

▷ The projected growth rate of this occupation is 44 percent, making it one of the fastest-growing occupations in the country. As the technology improves, sonography is being used more and more as a diagnostic tool. As the population ages, there will be more need for medical testing.
▷ Many doctors and patients prefer sonograms to other diagnostic tools, which can be invasive or can involve exposure to radiation.

Diagnostic medical sonographers use imaging equipment to direct sound waves into a patient's body in order to diagnose medical problems or conditions. This procedure is known as an ultrasound, sonogram, or echocardiogram. Good traits to have for this profession include attention to detail and excellent hand-eye coordination and interpersonal skills. Sonographers specialize in many different parts of the body. Here are a few examples:

▷ Abdominal sonographers image the abdomen and nearby organs, such as the kidney and liver.
▷ Breast sonographers image breast tissues. They can screen for breast cancer or track tumors in women with breast cancer.
▷ Obstetric and gynecologic sonographers image the female reproductive system. Most everyone has seen ultrasound images of a friend or family member's developing fetus. These pictures were probably imaged and printed by a diagnostic medical sonographer.

All types of medical sonographers prepare patients for procedures by taking a medical history and operating the sonogram equipment, which involves pressing an instrument called an ultrasound transducer against the parts of the body that need to be imaged. The transducer emits sound, which bounces back and creates images that the sonographer can view on a screen, record, and print out. Most diagnostic medical sonographers work in hospitals.

The majority of diagnostic medical sonographers have two-year associate degrees. One-year certificate programs are also available, but these are usually for people who are already medical professionals, such as nurses. Associate degree programs focus on medical terminology, anatomy, and how to interpret sonographic images. Programs usually focus on a specialty, such as those listed above.

Most employers prefer to hire certified sonographers. Certification can be earned by completing an accredited program and passing an exam. A few states require sonographers to be licensed.

For more information on diagnostic medical sonographers, visit the website for the Society of Diagnostic Medical Sonography, www.sdms .org. For information on finding an associate degree or certificate program, see chapter 6 or visit the website for the Commission on Accreditation of Allied Health Education Programs, www.caahep.org.

If you've decided to pursue an associate degree, chapter 6 can help you find the right community, vocational, or technical college. Chapters 7, 8, and 9 can help with your school applications, and chapter 10 will give you information on how to pay for this additional education. Putting in those extra two years can be the best investment you ever make.

Outlook for Jobs Requiring an Associate Degree, 2010-2020

Jobs for which an associate degree is the most significant source of postsecondary education or training.

Occupation	Employment (in thousands)		Employment Change		Jobs Growth/ Replacement 2010-2020 (in thousands)	2010 Median Annual Wages
	2010	2020	No. (in thousands)	%		
Funeral service managers, directors, morticians, and undertakers	29.3	34.6	5.3	18.2	10.7	$54,330
Paralegals and legal assistants	256.0	302.9	46.9	18.3	83.4	$46,680
Respiratory therapists	112.7	143.9	31.2	27.7	52.7	$54,280
Occupational therapist assistants	28.5	40.8	12.3	43.3	16.8	$51,010
Dental hygienists	181.8	250.3	68.5	37.7	104.9	$68,250
Diagnostic medical sonographers	53.7	77.1	23.4	43.5	31.7	$64,380

Source: Bureau of Labor Statistics Selected Occupational Projections Data, http://data.bls.gov/oep.

SIX

Getting the Training and Education You Need

Where Should You Look?

You looked into your chosen career. And you see that you'll need a certificate or an associate degree to pursue it. Or maybe you've decided to go into a trade and would like to find the right apprenticeship program. Or perhaps you've decided to start your own business and want to take a few classes. Taking one or more classes is a great way to learn new skills. There are many good reasonably priced options for all of these.

This chapter is organized by the training and education categories mentioned in the previous chapters and will tell you how to get required training and education for the job you want. It will also help you find classes that may not be required but will be helpful in your career. If you are still unsure what kind of training you will need, go back to chapters 2 through 5 or refer to the Occupational Outlook Handbook. Come back to this chapter to get information on where to go from there.

Apprenticeships

The good news about apprenticeships is that you will almost always get paid to train. In addition, your apprenticeship program or employer may pay for any classes you need outside the program.

The U.S. Department of Labor has developed an extensive network of apprenticeship programs and provides many easy and convenient ways to find the right one for you. Trades are so important to our national economy and infrastructure that there is even a U.S. Office of Apprenticeship, which develops and registers apprenticeships. Here is how the U.S. Department of Labor describes its Registered Apprenticeship program:

Registered Apprenticeship programs meet the skilled workforce needs of American industry, training millions of qualified individuals for lifelong careers since 1937. Registered Apprenticeship helps mobilize America's workforce with structured, on-the-job learning in traditional industries such as construction and manufacturing, as well as new emerging industries such as health care, information technology, energy, telecommunications, and more. Registered Apprenticeship connects job seekers looking to learn new skills with employers looking for qualified workers resulting in a workforce with industry-driven training and employers with a competitive edge.

The Registered Apprenticeship program offers access to 1,000 career areas. With a Registered Apprenticeship you receive:

▸ **A paycheck.** From day one, you will earn a paycheck guaranteed to increase over time as you learn new skills.
▸ **Hands-on career training.** As an apprentice, you will receive practical on-the-job training in a wide selection of programs, such as health care, construction, information technology, and geospatial careers.
▸ **An education.** You'll receive hands-on training and have the potential to earn college credit, even an associate or bachelor's degree, in many cases paid for by your employer.
▸ **A career.** Once you complete your apprenticeship, you will be on your way to a successful long-term career with a competitive salary, and little or no education debt.
▸ **National industry certification.** When you graduate from a career training program, you'll be certified and can take your certification anywhere in the United States
▸ **Recognizable partners.** Many of the nation's most recognizable companies, such as CVS/pharmacy and UPS, have Registered Apprenticeship programs.

Applicants for apprenticeships must be at least sixteen years old and meet the program sponsor's qualifications. They also must demonstrate to the sponsor that they have the ability and aptitude to master the fundamentals of the occupation and complete the required instruction.

Apprenticeships last anywhere from two to eight years, with the average being four. As you become more experienced in the trade or occupation, your salary will increase.

To apply for an apprenticeship, use one of the websites in the "How Do I Find an Apprenticeship?" box to locate an opportunity you're interested in. Either contact the apprenticeship program directly, or check with the national Office of Apprenticeship or your state apprenticeship office. You can also contact a labor union in the trade or field you want to enter. To find contact information for these organizations, click on the links provided in the box. Or simply stop by a One-Stop Career Center for guidance on the application process (to find one near you, visit www .servicelocator.org/onestopcenters.asp).

How Do I Find an Apprenticeship?

There are several easy ways to find apprenticeship programs in the trade or field you're interested in.

CareerOneStop's apprenticeship locator (enter zip code or city/state): http://maps.servicelocator.org/education/apprenticeship.aspx

Apprenticeship Program Sponsors Database (select state and county): http://oa.doleta.gov/bat.cfm?start

List of State Apprenticeship Websites (click on state link): www.doleta .gov/oa/sainformation.cfm

State Offices of Apprenticeship: www.doleta.gov/oa/stateoffices.cfm

Office of Apprenticeship List of Officially Recognized Apprenticeable Occupations: www.iowaworkforce.org/apprenticeship/ apprenticeableoccupations.pdf

Union Directory (enter union name, city and state, or zip): www.unions.org

Receive information about unions in your area (fill out form): www .unions.org/apprenticeships.php

To read more about apprenticeships, visit the Office of Apprenticeship's information page at www.doleta.gov/oa/apprentices_new.cfm. Still not sure about whether you want to apply for an apprenticeship? Read apprenticeship success stories on the 21st Century Apprenticeship website, https://21stcenturyapprenticeship.workforce3one.org.

Certificates and Associate Degrees

As you read in chapters 4 and 5, you can get a great career with a certificate or a two-year degree. These options cost money, but they are still much less expensive than four-year degrees. Many people work at a job while they earn their certificate or associate degree, but there are other ways to finance your education and training. See chapter 10 for information on training and education costs, personal resources, and financial aid.

Certificates

The Occupational Outlook Handbook defines *certificate* this way: "An award for demonstrating competency in a skill or set of skills, typically through the passage of an examination, work experience, training, or some combination thereof. Certification is always voluntary. Some certification programs may require a certain level of educational achievement for eligibility."

Where Will I Earn My Certificate?

Some certifications require classes, usually at a community or career college, to earn a certificate; others require self-paced study, on-the-job training, and an exam. The following links will give you all the information about what you'll need to do to get the certificate you want.

Career OneStop Short-Term Training Finder (enter occupation, school, or program and state or zip): www.careerinfonet.org/shorttermtraining

Career OneStop Certificate Finder (enter certification name, certifying organization, occupation, or industry): www.acinet.org/certifications_new

College Navigator (enter one or more of many search options): http://nces.ed.gov/collegenavigator

---

Certificates are often offered at career training schools, community colleges, vocational schools or academies, and technical colleges. Many times, there are on-campus or online options for these certificate programs, and these may be completed much more quickly than the associate degree.

Other certificates are offered through a national or state accreditation organization and require that you study for and take an exam; it also may require you to do on-the-job training while studying to take your certification exam.

To find a certificate program, see "Where Will I Earn My Certificate?" If your certificate requires college or career school classes, you will have to apply for admission to the school. Chapters 7, 8, and 9 can help you through this process. You will also have to pay tuition, fees, and other expenses, depending on whether you are working a job while going to school or living at home. See chapter 10 for information about training costs, personal resources, and financial aid.

Associate Degrees

Associate degrees can be earned in business, information technology, health services, early childhood education, engineering, and many other career fields. There are more than 2,000 schools in the United States that award associate degrees.

Associate degrees are most often earned at community colleges, technical colleges, junior colleges, or career training schools, but can also be offered at four-year universities. They can be completed on campus or online. To earn your associate degree, you will typically have to complete 60 college credits. It usually takes the average full-time student two years to do this, but for part-time working students, it may take longer. For an internship and other types of programs, you may earn classroom credit. Many colleges also give credit for some types of military training and experience and for portfolios that demonstrate skills learned on the job.

To find an associate degree program that's right for you, see "Where Will I Earn My Associate Degree?" For tips on applying to a school to get your associate degree, see chapters 7, 8, and 9. Expenses for your associate degree will include tuition, textbooks, travel, and more, depending on whether you are working a job or living at home. For information on costs and financial aid, see chapter 10.

Where Will I Earn My Associate Degree?

Perhaps you want to attend your local community college and don't need to look elsewhere, but if you are interested in moving to another location or are interested in a course of study that your local college doesn't offer, there are many ways to find one that fits your needs.

CareerOneStop Short-Term Training Finder (enter occupation or course of study): www.careerinfonet.org/edutraining

College Navigator (enter one or more of many search options): http://uces.ed.gov/collegenavigator

---

Taking the Occasional Class (for Occupations That Require No Formal Training)

You don't need to take a test to see if you need a class. No matter your interests or needs, you probably need to take a class to learn more. Learn something that you want to learn or learn things that will make you a better employee or help you earn more at your current job.

For example, if you work with computers in your job, you might want to get the latest Microsoft certification by taking several computer classes, or you might want to take a class in the latest accounting software to help you keep track of expenses for your new business. Whatever you do for a living, you'll want to take a class now and then to keep up your skills or learn new ones.

You can choose from online classes and in-person classes. You can even find one-on-one classes if you want the instructor all to yourself. No matter what classes you take, you'll want to find ones that meet your needs without emptying your wallet.

Free Classes

You can find free online and one-on-one training for your small business from a Small Business Development Center (SBDC). Visit the Association of Small Business Development Centers website, www.asbcd-us.org, to find your local SBDC. You can also find free training (or training for a very small fee) at your local library. Community centers, senior centers, and jobs centers offer free classes to people who are looking for a job. You need to check with the centers near you to see if you have to live within a certain district or earn below a certain amount of money to qualify. Your local school district may also offer free classes to people who live within the district.

Reasonably Priced Classes

For classes at a reasonable fee, you cannot beat your local community college. They have for-credit classes and continuing education classes, so you can choose which one works best for you. In general, for-credit classes are more expensive, but they meet for a whole semester. When the class is over, you will have earned some credit hours that you can use toward a certificate or even a two-year degree. Continuing education classes usually meet for a shorter time and cost less. You often learn from an expert in the field, but the credits don't transfer.

You can also check out any local trade schools, community centers, and school districts to see if they offer classes. Some local businesses may also offer classes in specific software or business topics.

Barter: What's Old Is New Again

If you are low on cash, you can often barter to get a service you need. Although it's an old system, bartering goods and services with someone else is a great way to save money while getting something you want in return.

For example, I needed to learn how to use my new accounting software. The instruction book was several hundred pages long, and I'd already gone through the hour-long tutorial. Luckily, I had a business colleague who was a whiz at that particular software. He offered to give me several hours of his time as a one-on-one tutor if I would write some updated content for his website.

His suggestion gave me exactly what I needed, and it also gave him some much-needed content. And it didn't cost either of us a dime. So, if you need something that a local business owner can provide, consider bartering for a class or one-on-one tutoring.

Social Media for Dummies

Atlas Fishbeinner wanted to start his own business. He was a high school graduate with a natural genius for landscape design. He'd been mowing lawns during the summer since eighth grade, and his parent's yard (which he designed) was the highlight of the neighborhood.

His problem was that he didn't care much about communications technology. "I could e-mail my friends, but I didn't get why anybody would want to be on LinkedIn or even what it could do for me and my business. Luckily, I took a two-night course at my local community college. They explained everything and even gave me a workbook to help me plan my social media campaign."

"Now, people all over my city 'like' me on Facebook, and my lawnscaping designs are featured on both my website and my LinkedIn page. My next goal is to be featured in *Entrepreneur* magazine as a young business owner to watch."

Best Bets for Cheap Business Classes

Your best bet for cheap business classes is almost certainly your local community college. The community college usually offers the largest number and widest variety of classes to the community. If you have a four-year college or university in the vicinity, you may want to check their catalog as well. However, four-year schools are often not interested in offering classes for the community. Their main concern is training students and helping those students get their four-year degrees.

Your local library is another great place to take business-related classes—and to find classes offered in the area. Organizations that offer classes often put sign-up sheets or informational posters in the library in order to get students. In addition, you can ask your local librarian for information about career or business coaches, advanced training opportunities, or one-on-one training. In addition, check at your library for audiovisual options such as DVD or video classes on basic business subjects or on starting your own business.

Last but certainly not least, try your local Small Business Development Center. To find one in your area, visit the website for the Association of Small Business Development Centers, www.absdc-us.org.

Best Bets for Cheap Computer Classes

Computers are updated frequently, and new software comes out almost every day. To keep up with all of this technology, you probably need one or more computer classes. Here's where to look to find the largest variety of classes at the best price.

Community College

Your local community college is an excellent resource for computer classes. Most campuses have at least one computer lab, and many community colleges do the training for local businesses as well as for their

---

The Basics: Small Business in a Nutshell

If you want to start your own small business, you don't need to go to college, but you do need to have practical knowledge of a variety of business processes to be successful. The SBDC can help, but you also need to think about all the various skills you will need to run your own business. You may need a class or at least a seminar for the ones that you don't know anything about, including the following:

- Accounting
- Marketing
- Public relations
- Taxes
- Human resources/hiring/firing/employee relations
- Long-term planning/goal setting
- Management training
- Computers
- Customer service
- Media
- Social media/online marketing/web marketing

You may know a little about many of these, but you will need some help with managing the day-to-day activities of the business and the long-term goal setting that it takes to be successful.

Taking one or more classes can help you be more successful as a business owner and even give you the training you'll want in order to grow your business. As your business gets bigger, you'll need to learn more to be able to manage the business, such as how to cultivate and retain employees and how to create your own franchise to sell to others.

students and the community. You can go to the school's website to find its online catalog of classes, or the school may mail out a catalog to everyone within its district.

Library

Your local library may offer computer and other technology classes. You can check the library's website or go to the main office or branch. If your library does not offer classes, the librarians may know of good low-cost options for you. You can also suggest that they start offering classes to the public.

If you are just starting out, you probably don't have money to hire a marketing or public relations firm to help you market your small business. So taking a marketing class can be a good idea. However, you don't need Marketing 101. You need a class geared specifically to marketing a small business.

Check your local library and nearby community colleges for these classes. You can also check out the SBDC in your region. It may offer classes, or it can point you to the nearest organization that does.

Community Centers, Senior Centers, and Job Centers

Check out these options to see if they offer computer classes. In most cases, it may depend on what exactly you want to learn about computers. If you have little experience with them, these organizations can be a great way to familiarize yourself with computers and what they can do. Also, don't discount today's senior centers. Many offer classes to the community no matter what the age of the participants. Local job centers also offer training for people within the district. If they don't offer training, they usually know where you can find training at reasonable prices or even free of charge.

SEVEN

Applications and Essays

How to Succeed

Filling out school and training program applications can be time-consuming and just a little scary. But you don't have to be a rocket scientist to fill out the forms and get the letters to your school or training program on time. All you have to do is keep an eye on the deadlines and proceed step-by-step to complete the application and send the requested documents. The tips and advice in this chapter are geared toward applications for schools or training programs, but many of the basic concepts can also be used while completing a job application.

Elements of an Application

Your application packet may include only the application or a whole variety of materials that you will have to gather. Many schools require letters of recommendation or extra forms besides the application. Training programs often require only an application. In this section, we review what you usually need.

Focus on Programs That Interest You Most

Experts advise students applying to schools to choose six or seven. Applying to more than that is usually a waste of time and money. The same goes for students interested in training programs or schools for training.

Applying to more than six or seven schools wastes time because getting all the pieces, such as letters of recommendation, the application, the essay, and your transcripts ready can take several weeks even if you're quick. In addition, some schools and training programs charge an application fee. That can add up if you apply to twenty programs. Talk to your high school counselor about training programs or local schools you are interested in attending. A counselor can help you narrow down your choices or help you find more information.

Application Fee

Before you apply, go to the website of the school or program and check to see if it costs to apply. Application fees typically range from $25 to $80.

Application Form

Most schools and training programs have some kind of formal application. Luckily, these days most of them are online. In fact, you can probably apply online for most schools and training programs.

The application form will usually ask for the following:

- Personal data, such as name, contact information, date of birth, social security number, citizenship information, and ethnic background (which is usually optional)
- Educational data: location and name of the high school you attended or are attending and any programs you've completed or classes you've taken past or outside of high school
- Test scores, if applicable
- Family information
- Extracurricular and volunteer activities
- Work experience

Extracurricular activities can include any outside activity you've taken part in, not just school-sponsored activities like sports. Work experience is impressive to anyone reading your application and can include everything from waiting tables to a summer job as a lifeguard at the local pool. If you worked during high school, make sure to include the job in your application.

Depending on the program or school, you may be asked for a resume. A resume is so important to your later working life that there is an entire chapter in this book devoted to writing one. If the application you're filling out requires a resume, see chapter 8. One caveat: before you submit your online application, print or make a copy of it for your records. You will need to update and use it, or a version of it, throughout your working life.

High School Transcript

Schools usually want an official copy of your high school transcript. This means that the transcript must be sent directly from your high school to the school in a sealed envelope. If you studied for and passed a GED test, you will most likely need to have a transcript of your GED scores sent to the school.

Test Scores

Some schools require that you provide them with ACT or SAT scores before they will consider you for admission. You can go through the ACT or SAT website to have your scores sent to the schools you want to attend. Check with the schools to see which accept SAT and which accept ACT. Schedule these tests as soon as you can in your senior year so that the scores can be sent to the schools you choose.

Many community colleges don't require either test, but you usually can take it and submit the scores for advanced placement. Many trade schools require the Career Programs Assessment (CPAt), which tests fundamental reading, writing, and math skills. Trade school programs at community colleges may use the Computer-Adaptive Placement Assessment and Support System (COMPASS) or the ACT.

You will most likely have to take some type of assessment test so that the community or technical college can know where you're "at" in terms of the skills that will be necessary to complete the program. The same is true for most training programs and trade schools.

Letters of Recommendation

Many programs and schools require that you get three letters of recommendation from adults who know you, your schoolwork, and your career goals. The most important point here is to start early. When you ask people to write a recommendation for you, give them two to four weeks to write the letter.

Finding the Right Person

Think carefully about which people to ask. First, make sure you know how many letters are required for each school or program you plan to apply to. In most cases, you will need three, and you can use the same letter for all the schools you wish to attend.

You can ask a teacher, your counselor, your boss at work, a minister from your church, or some other adult who knows you well. You can't ask a family member. Create a list of the three people you'd like to ask and include a second choice for each one in case your first choice doesn't have time to write a letter for you.

Asking for a Recommendation

Approach each person and ask if he or she has time to write a letter of recommendation for you. If anyone doesn't have time, thank her or him and move on to your second choice. If someone says yes, be prepared with the information from the school or program and a stamped envelope for the recommender to send the letter in. As well as being stamped, the envelope should already be addressed to the school or program. Remember to tell the recommender if the letter needs to be on school letterhead or any other requirements from the school you're applying to.

Many schools and training programs also accept letters of recommendation online. You might need to give your recommender a website address and a code or password to get in. Many recommenders will find this option more convenient.

Here's the key to asking for recommendations: don't be shy. Recommenders who are teachers or counselors will be used to writing these letters, and most people who have never been asked to provide a recommendation letter will be flattered you asked.

Helping the Recommender

Teachers and other school personnel are frequently asked to write recommendation letters, so most of them know what to do. If you have asked your employer (or someone else who has no experience with this type of letter), you can offer that person some facts about you, your extracurricular activities, and your career goals. This information can help the person write a good letter about you.

After the Letter Is Sent

After the letters are written and sent, write thank-you notes to everyone who wrote a letter for you. Don't copy the same text over for each person. If these people can write a whole letter about you, you can write a few personalized sentences to express how much you appreciate their help with your application.

Interviews

Even if you live far from the school you want to attend, it can be a good idea to ask for an interview. With today's technology, you can set up a video interview with the admissions office. If you don't have access to this technology, consult with your school librarian to see if you can use their resources to make this happen online. If possible, agree to meet with an alum from that school or go to the school in person to interview.

Application Essay

Some schools and training programs ask you to write an essay along with your application. This is a big job, and an important one, so we take a detailed look at it in the next section. The typical essay for an application like this is usually pretty short—one to two pages double-spaced—so it won't be like writing a research paper for school.

Writing the Admissions Essay

The admissions teams at most schools and training programs have been reading admissions essays from prospective students for years. Those years of experience help them craft ever more telling questions for applicants.

Telling? Yes. They want to find out which students really want to attend their school and which students are applying just to say they were accepted. The types of questions that admissions folks think up fall into these three categories:

▸ **What would you like to write about?** This type of question lets you choose your own question or suggests only the broadest idea for you to narrow down as you will. Actually, this type of question isn't easy at all. It can be more difficult because you need to narrow down a broad theme or choose a topic that you can write about in a limited number of words.

▸ **You chose us because . . . ?** This question type asks students why they have chosen this particular school or training program in the first place. The question seems easy at the outset, but it's even trickier than making you choose your own question. You want to impress the admissions team with your reasons for choosing their school and not repeat what everyone else has said. That means you probably need to do some research about the special characteristics of the school and know what you plan to do with the training once it's completed. A librarian at your local public library or your school librarian can help you with this. Your high school counselor will also be a good source of information about how to go about this.

▸ **Tell us about yourself.** This type of essay prompt is common and can be difficult. You want to tell them why you would be a wonderful addition to their school or program while also giving some personal information about yourself. If you err by giving too much of one or the other, your essay will be bogged down. Balance is key to making the most of this type of question. Be yourself and not who you think the admissions committee wants you to be. Honesty is an impressive quality, and experienced essay readers can tell when an applicant isn't being genuine.

Need Help with Essay Writing? Ask a Librarian

If you are worried about writing your application essay, go to your local library and ask for help. Your librarian can put you in touch with excellent reference sources such as Sarah Myers McGinty's *The College Application Essay*, now in its fifth edition (College Board, 2012). Your librarian can find sample essays for you, books containing sample essay questions from major training programs, and tips to make your writing sparkle. You can also visit your library's web page to find resources to help you write a winning essay that will take the admissions team by storm.

Before You Write

Brainstorm before you begin writing the essay. You can make a list or ask your friends to help you think of good topics that will showcase what is unique about you. Look at some sample essays, but don't try to pattern your essay after anyone else's work. It needs to be original.

Above all, start early! Don't wait until the last minute to write your admissions essay. Do it early and then take the time to rewrite it until it shines. The goal here isn't to write the application essay seconds before it's due. Your goal is to finish the essay at least a week before it needs to be e-mailed or two weeks before you have to snail-mail it. So start early, and spend some extra time rewriting.

As You Write

Give yourself plenty of time to write the rough draft. Don't do it at the last minute. Write down everything you can think of that might apply to your topic. You can always edit it out later if the piece is too long. Pay attention to the rules from your school. Some colleges want essays to be a specific word count or page count, which is usually fairly brief. Do not send more or less than is asked for. If your essay is too long, they may not read all of it.

▹ **Choose a topic that's personal to you and not too broad.** You want to cover only one topic and cover it well. One error students make is trying to cover too much ground in their essays. Instead, stick to one small topic and cover it thoroughly. You are trying to show the admissions team what kind of person you are, not report everything you've ever learned in your life.

▹ **Use specific examples.** Another rookie mistake is to talk in generalities in your essay. Use specific concrete examples. For example, if you want to write about overcoming obstacles in your life, be specific about what you did. Did you overcome your fear of heights and conquer the balance beam in gym class? Did you overcome your terror of public speaking by giving a speech? Are there financial or other personal obstacles that you've had to overcome in your life that you feel comfortable writing about?

▸ **Be sincere.** Don't write about things that you don't care about. Choose a topic that actually matters to you. And don't say things in your essay that you don't mean.

▸ **Don't use $10 words.** Many students think they will impress the admissions committee by using big words. That doesn't work. Instead, use words that you understand and make sense to you. If you use words that you don't normally use, it's too easy to misuse one.

Break Time and Help with the Rewrite

Write your first draft and then take a break. Very few people can write an essay and then edit it right away. Give yourself time to forget what you wrote. If possible, give yourself at least a week before you try to edit the essay. Go out with friends, watch television, read a book, play a video game—whatever you like to do. Give yourself at least 24 hours before you try to edit your writing.

Ask your favorite English teacher to help you with your essay. He or she can help you edit or even suggest a good topic for you. Your English

---

The Best Websites for Sample Admissions Essays and Advice

This sample essay on QuintCareers is an example of using simple language and one simple idea to create a great essay: www.quintcareers .com/collegegate4.html. If you read only one sample essay, this is the one. The story about the writer's work on a local youth board is an excellent example of how to impress the admissions team. You also want to read the critique of another sample essay for tips about your own work: http:// collegeapps.about.com/od/essays/a/EssayYouthBoard.htm.

The College Board offers two slideshows on its website that give terrific advice on application essays, "8 Tips for Crafting Your Best College Essays" and "3 Ways to Approach Common College Essay Questions." You can find them, along with articles and videos to make you feel more prepared to write an essay if you need to, at https://bigfuture.collegeboard. org/get-in/essays.

teacher can even point you toward sample essays that may spark a good idea or books that may help you edit your writing.

Proofread, Proofread, Proofread

I cannot say this enough. Proofread your essay. You don't want any typos in your essay. Proofread the essay yourself first and then ask a friend to read it. Proof your writing more than once to make sure that you catch any typos. Don't rely totally on your software's spelling and grammar checker.

It might help you keep track of all that you need to do when applying to training programs and schools to fill out and update the Training/School Application Tracker at the end of this chapter as you go through the process.

Not all training programs require an essay. However, for programs with small enrollment or tough standards, an essay is a way to differentiate between students who really want to be in the program and those who don't.

For the best results, write an essay tailored to the application that requires it. Some scholarships and grants also require an essay, so you may be able to use your admissions essay to win a scholarship or grant.

I've Been Accepted by Three Programs—Now What?

First, pat yourself on the back for being accepted by more than one school. Celebrate a little with your friends. Then, it's time to make a decision.

Follow these four steps to narrow your choices down to the best one for you:

1. Get advice from your family, friends, and advisors. Ask the people you trust about your choices. Don't forget to talk to your high school counselor and high school teachers.
2. Compare the schools or programs. Which ones have the best facilities for what you want to learn?

3. Go to each school. You may be surprised at how different you feel about the school once you're there. Can you see yourself walking from class to class?
4. Alert the schools to your answer. Remember, there is no one school for you. Many schools can be the right one for you, depending on what you are looking for. Once you've made a decision, send your acceptance and no-thank-you answers back to the schools. Many training programs have a deadline for you to give them your answer.

If you've been accepted into an apprenticeship program, you will likely be paid for your training. But if you've applied to a trade or vocational school or community college, your next step will be to find a way to pay for it. See chapter 10 to explore your options. Whether you are entering a training program to receive a certificate or enrolling in a community college to earn your associate degree, you will be surprised at the number of ways you can finance your education.

Training/School Application Tracker

	Training Program 1	Training Program 2	Training Program 3
Application Package			
Sent application form e-mail/mail?			
Application fee?			
Application deadline			
Sent transcripts?			
Test Scores			
Sent SAT scores			
Sent ACT scores			
Sent misc. scores			
Sent misc. scores			
Letters of Recommendation			
Person writing letter 1?			
Sent thank-you note?			
Person writing letter 2?			
Sent thank-you note?			
Person writing letter 3?			
Sent thank-you note?			
Other Requirements			
Application essay sent?			
Telephone screen date/time?			

cont.

Training/School Application Tracker (cont.)

	Training Program 1	Training Program 2	Training Program 3
In-person interview date/ time			
In-person interview, sent thank-you note?			
Financial Aid			
Financial aid form deadline			
FAFSA sent online/mail?			
Special training program aid form sent?			
Special state aid form sent?			
RESULTS			
Not-admitted letter rec'd			
Wait-list letter rec'd			
Admitted letter rec'd			
Financial aid letter rec'd			
Deadline to accept admission			
Deadline to accept financial aid offer			
"No thanks" sent to other schools or training programs			

EIGHT

Resumes

Showing Them What You Know

Whether it's for an application to a training program or school, or for a job application, just about everyone will have to create a resume at some point in their life. Don't be intimidated when you start your resume. There are some basic things to consider that will make the process much easier.

Like almost everything else, resumes have a fashion and a style. They also have a sell-by date. The old-fashioned resumes your parents (or brothers and sisters) wrote won't work for you now. These days, the main formats for resumes are chronological, functional, and hybrid.

> ▶ **Chronological.** As the name implies, the chronological resume lists your work history in order: the most recent job goes first, then the next most recent job, and so on. This is the most common type of resume. This format works best for people who have a lot of job experience or job experience that shows a progression from lower-level jobs to higher-level jobs. Use this type of resume to show how good you are at learning what is required on the job and that you get promoted because you are good at what you do.

▷ **Functional.** A functional resume uses the same information as the chronological resume, but it is organized to show everything you are good at. The idea here is to downplay your lack of a work history or a spotty work history. Organize this resume with a section on skills, accomplishments, or achievements at the top. In this section, you can highlight what you can do and what you've done successfully in the past. This type of resume works best for recent graduates or those just out of the military, those who are changing careers (and therefore need training in the new area), and people with a spotty work history or long gaps between jobs.

> ### CV 101
>
> If you are applying for training, you may run into the term "CV" instead of "resume." *CV* stands for *curriculum vitae,* a Latin phrase that means "the course of (one's) life." In most cases, a CV has much more detail than your average resume. CVs usually include both professional and academic accomplishments.
>
> For more information about how to create a CV, visit www.career.vt .edu/resumeguide/vitae.html.

▷ **Hybrid.** A hybrid resume is just what it sounds like: a cross between a functional resume and a chronological one. In short, you use whichever parts of the other two types of resumes work best for your specific situation. Maybe you list your job experience chronologically but start with a list of skills or accomplishments. This type of resume has become quite popular recently and can help you showcase what's interesting and unique about you and your job skills.

Anatomy of a Resume

Although it probably seems complex, a resume is really a fairly simple document. There are just two parts: what is required and what is optional. Despite what many people will tell you, there are only three items in the required part of your resume. The optional sections actually outnumber the requirements. The key is to make sure that your required sections are clearly marked and easy to read. Another important point is to be careful about how many optional sections you add. Resumes need to be short.

Required

First, your resume must have a heading that includes your name, a telephone number, and an e-mail address. Most people also include their postal address. This text is usually organized as a block or centered as if it were letterhead. It doesn't matter how you do it, but you must include basic contact information.

Second, you need to include some of your work history. You don't have to include every job you've ever had, but you need to include something. If you don't have any job experience, you can list volunteer activities. You probably need to be clear that they were volunteer opportunities and not paying jobs. However, you aren't required to differentiate intern positions from paid jobs.

The last requirement for your resume is your education. List any education or certificates you have earned. That's a given. You can list college courses you've taken if you didn't get a degree. You don't have to list every single course title, but it can be helpful to show how many hours you have taken in each subject area. Also, if you will be graduating in the near future, mention that in your resume.

The Key to Keywords

When your resume is received by a potential employer, it will be scanned—by either a human or a software program—for keywords. If your resume doesn't include enough keywords, or the right keywords, it won't even make the first cut.

Try to work in keywords mentioned in the job description for a job you're applying for. A good place to do this is the "Skills" section.

For example, if you are applying for a position as a receptionist, your resume may be scanned for the following words and phrases: *receptionist, telephone skills, friendly, computer skills, people person, able to multitask, professional appearance, deals well with difficult people.* Other good keywords would be the names of software programs or credentials specified in the job posting.

Tailor the Resume for the Position

You do not have to include every single job you've ever had on your resume. For example, if you are seeking an apprentice position in a union, don't list all the waiting on tables you did during high school. On the other hand, you should note that you volunteered for Habitat for Humanity and helped to build houses, especially if the trade you are applying for is carpentry, plumbing, or something similar. You can also include work you may have done in your uncle's plumbing business.

If your old jobs can highlight why you would be an excellent choice for an internship, an apprenticeship, or a scholarship, list them. If any of them shows something good about you that will help you get what you are seeking, keep it in the resume. If it's just filler, leave it out.

Optional

You can include any of the following sections in your resume:

▷ **Career objective.** Some people swear that this is a requirement, but it's not. If you'd like to list a career objective (finding a challenging position that utilizes my carpentry skills, for example), feel free.

▷ **Honors or extracurricular activities.** If you have just graduated, you probably want to list any honors or activities on your resume. Sports and other group activities look good because they show how you've learned teamwork.

▷ **Volunteer work.** Include any volunteer work you've done. This looks even better than honors or school activities. Admissions committees like to give scholarships and admission to people who are well rounded. Helping less fortunate people is a good way to be a better person and appeal to admissions folk. *A word of advice:* If you don't have any volunteer experience, go out and get some. If possible, volunteer for something related to the field you want to enter.

▷ **Professional honors.** List any honors you've earned while at work, such as employee of the month. Anything that can show leadership skills is a good thing to include on a resume.

▷ **Special skills.** List any special skills, such as knowledge of specific software programs, your typing speed, or anything else that makes you valuable. Don't include hobbies. You may have

> ## What If I Don't Have Any Work Experience?
>
> You can always find something to put on your resume to showcase how responsible, organized, and motivated you are. All of the traits that make you a good employee or volunteer can also highlight you as a good candidate for financial aid, an internship, or admittance to a training program.
>
> If you don't have work experience, use your volunteer experience. Start with any volunteer experience that relates to the reason you are creating a resume. But if you run out of relevant volunteer experience, use any volunteer gig to show how responsible you are.
>
> Don't be afraid to use internships or other "joblike" experience in your resume. You can even list running your own business, no matter how small, since this shows initiative, which resume readers like. As a last resort, list extracurricular activities, especially sports, on your resume. Demonstrating teamwork can be a good way to show responsibility and good people skills to anyone reviewing your resume.

heard about the use of keywords in websites. This is a good section in which to make use of them. According to search engine optimization experts, you need to embed keywords in your web page in order to get the attention of search engines such as Google. Along the same lines, some resume experts claim that you need to do the same thing to catch the interest of human resource professionals. The truth is that many human resource offices are so busy that they use a computer to scan and "read" resumes. The computer rejects those that don't include the right keywords somewhere in the text. Try to work in keywords that you think the program scanning your resume might be looking for, such as important words from the job description for the job you're applying for.

E-resumes

These days, most people have two electronic versions of each of their many resumes. One version is formatted, so it looks good. This version gets printed out for in-person interviews and gets mailed to schools and

10 Tips for Unblocking Resume Roadblocks

Resume writing, especially that first resume, can be difficult and time-consuming. To make sure you get through it intact, follow these rules:

1. Look at sample resumes to get ideas. It's so much easier to create your own resume when you can look at examples and see what you like and don't like. Check out books on resume writing from your library, or look at samples online. One site to visit is WetFeet (www.wetfeet.com).

2. Dump all the information for your work history and education into a word processing document. Double-check the dates, titles, and details of each job position, your education, grade point average, and other information; then save that document.

3. Write to your specific audience. How will your history translate to learning something new at the school, training program, or profession you hope to enter?

4. Create some sections, such as "Special Skills," and brainstorm all your skills and abilities. Fill these sections.

5. Edit. Keep the writing concise and action-oriented. Focus on specific accomplishments or responsibilities. You don't have to use complete sentences; bulleted lists of statements work well.

6. Format. Once you feel you have a complete draft, format the document so that it is visually appealing.

7. Proofread. The importance of this step can't be overemphasized.

8. Bug a friend. Ask at least one other person to review your resume and proofread it again.

9. Bug an English teacher. Ask an English teacher or a friend who is good at writing to give your resume one last look.

10. Save your final document and prepare to revise a version for each school, job, or training program you apply for. Now you won't have to reinvent the wheel the next time an opportunity comes along that you want to apply for.

> Most experts advise you to create a "master" resume with all your jobs and information in it—the "kitchen sink" version, in other words. Then, when you find a program or school you want to apply to, you use the pieces from your master document that best fit the requirements of the position you want.
>
> So, for example, if you want to apply to a program that trains X-ray technicians, who work directly with the public, you can highlight your vast experience working part-time at retail jobs with the public and include any awards such as employee of the month or promotions based on your excellent customer service.

training programs. The other version is called *plain text* because it isn't formatted. This version is used if you need to copy and paste your resume, or parts of it, to a training program, company, or school website. Usually you won't need to do that, but some organizations may require it.

You want to be ready for whatever the organization asks, so it's good to have your resume ready both with and without formatting.

Formatted

You've written a solid draft of your resume in a word processing program such as Microsoft Word. Print it out on good-quality white (or off-white) paper. Always have a crisp, clean copy or two ready at an in-person interview. Your school may also ask you to snail-mail a copy of this resume to accompany your application.

Once you have your resume final and looking good, you can print it out and mail it or send it as an e-mail attachment—as either a Microsoft Word or a PDF document. If you use a word processing program other than Word, you should save it as a file type that anyone can open—and these days that means Word files, PDFs, or rich text files. One advantage of PDFs is that they keep the resume's formatting and design intact but can still be searched electronically for keywords.

Unformatted

In addition to your carefully formatted resume, you should have a plain-text version—one that has all formatting and special characters stripped out. You will use this to copy and paste into the body of an e-mail or to

---

Good Resume Websites

Starting from scratch is almost always harder than seeing what other people have done before you, including making mistakes. The following websites provide advice from those with experience as well as good sample resumes to review.

What NOT to Do: 7 Ways to Ruin Your Resume
If you don't look at anything else, read this article from CBS Money watch.com about resume mistakes and click on the link to the interactive critique of an actual resume. You'll learn more in ten minutes than you will by reading several books on the subject. http://shine.yahoo.com/work-money/what-not-to-do-7-ways-to-ruin-your-resume-2009803.html.

The Riley Guide
This site lists links to dozens of other sites that offer resume tips and advice as well as information about interviewing and how resume readers deal with and react to actual resumes. http://rileyguide.com/resprep.html.

The Damn Good Resume Website
If you want to choose from dozens of sample resumes from a wide variety of jobs, this is the website for you. There is also information about resume content and format as well as excellent advice about dealing with resume problems such as many short-term jobs or a long job gap. www.damngood.com.

Dummies.com Resumes
If you need to figure out which type of resume structure will work best for you and your goals, this is the place to find worthwhile descriptions and samples of all the most common types of resumes, including various hybrids. The site also tackles questions about video resumes, portfolio resumes, and key word resumes. www.dummies.com/how-to/business-careers/careers/Resumes.html.

---

copy and paste sections of it into an online application form. Save your formatted resume file as "plain text," an option on any word processing program. Open the file again and see what it looks like. Try to make it look as readable as possible without using any special formatting. It's permissible to use all-caps to indicate headings and asterisks to indicate bullet points in plain-text versions of your resume.

Need Resume Help? Ask a Librarian

If you're writing your first resume, the library is a great place to seek advice. Many libraries offer resume-writing workshops or even resume coaches to help you one-on-one with your resume.

If your local library doesn't offer workshops or coaches, ask the reference librarian for help finding recent books and online resources for resume writing. You may even find a local job networking group that meets weekly or monthly to help members write resumes and get jobs. Don't be afraid to go right up to the front desk and ask for help and resources. Librarians and library staff are there to help.

E-mailing Resumes

If your school, training program, or potential employer allows you to apply for admission online, it may also ask you to submit your resume the same way. Consider these tips before you e-mail.

▶ **Meet the requirements.** Double-check any details on *what* the organization requires from applicants and *how* it wishes to receive it. If possible, check the organization's website for information on preferred method. If the training program requests an attached file for the resume, does it specify file type? The program may want resumes submitted only as Microsoft Word documents, or as PDFs, or as plain text files, depending on its screening procedures.

▶ **Don't get blocked!** With today's sophisticated spam filters, many organizations' e-mail servers block all attachments from certain types of e-mail addresses—or they may block only certain types of attachments such as Zip files or PDFs.

▶ **Send two in one.** If a school or potential employer requests your resume as a Word document, PDF, or other attachment, your best bet is to attach it as requested but also copy and paste the plain-text version of it into the body of the e-mail, below your signature line. That way, if your attachment is not received, your resume will still be in their hands.

PDF to the Rescue

Sara Runnseleer had carefully written and edited her resume until it was perfect. She didn't want an errant software program to ruin all of her hard work.

"I knew that if I sent my resume to potential training programs as a Word file, it could look totally different, and wrong, depending on the program, even other versions of Word, people used to open it," Sara says. "I wanted my resume to look perfect online and on the printed page, so I made it into a PDF file. Now it can't be changed, and the formatting will be the same no matter who opens it."

These days, many software programs include the ability to save files as PDF documents. If your software does not have this capability, you can download free software called PDF Creator that allows you to convert a document easily into a PDF (for Windows systems only). It is available at http://sourceforge.net/projects/pdfcreator/.

▶ **Choose your subject line carefully.** The subject line—the text that appears in the receiver's in-box—should be a clear indication of why you're sending an e-mail.

▶ **Be savvy about attachment names.** If you're sending your resume as an e-mail attachment, make sure you name it so that it's easily identifiable. *Yourlastname_resume.doc* is your best bet—and be sure to include the extension .doc or .pdf so that it can be opened easily.

Custom Resumes

Once you have written your first resume, you will probably feel good that it's done. And you may be delighted that you never have to write another one. Oh, but you're wrong. You need to customize your resume for every school or training program that asks for it. (You'll also be doing this once you enter the job force and begin looking for your first job.)

Because you'll have different versions of each resume (don't forget the formatted and plain-text versions), you need a way to keep track of all the different versions. That's why you need to include resume versions in your job-search tracking system. There's a tracking sheet at the end of this chapter along with a resume-proofing checklist.

The Best Resume Books

Head to your local library and check out some books that can help you create your best resume.

Resume 101: A Student and Recent-Grad Guide to Crafting Resumes and Cover Letters That Land Jobs, by Quentin J. Schultze, foreword by Richard N. Bolles (Berkeley, CA: Ten Speed Press, 2011)

The Guide to Internet Job Searching, by Margaret Dikel and Frances Roehm (New York: McGraw-Hill, 2008)

McGraw-Hill's Big Red Book of Resumes (New York: McGraw-Hill, 2002)

The Complete Idiot's Guide to the Perfect Resume, by Susan Ireland (New York: Alpha Books, 2010)

Resume Magic, by Susan Britton Whitcomb (St. Paul, MN: JIST Works, 2010)

Resume Toolbox: Top Five Resume Mistakes

No matter what your friends say, you can never check your resume over too many times. One little typo can speak volumes about you and not say anything good. People who review resumes for training programs may think that you don't really care about getting into the program if you didn't care enough to proofread your application materials, including your resume.

According to Monster.com, these are the top five resume mistakes you need to avoid at all costs:

1. **Confusing organization.** Like web pages, resumes need to be easy to navigate. For this reason, many experts think you should use section titles such as Education, Skills, and Experience in your resume so that readers can easily skim the document and find what they want.

   In addition, don't use three or four different type styles or too many different type sizes to jazz up your resume. Jumbles of words in different type sizes and styles look confusing and don't invite reading. Experts suggest that you try to add as much white space as possible to your resume and stick with just one or two type styles.

2. **Wrong contact information.** Proofreading everything is important, but it's especially critical that all of your contact information be correct. How are potential training programs going to call or e-mail you if your contact information is wrong? You might be surprised at the number of people who don't proofread their address, phone number, or e-mail address because they are sure they typed it correctly the first time or forget that they moved last year.

3. **Wrong grammar, spelling, or punctuation.** Check and double-check every sentence on your resume. In fact, double-check this information yourself and then ask a friend to go over it again. If there are mistakes, those who review your resume will assume that you don't care about the training program you are applying for or, worse, don't know the correct grammar, spelling, or punctuation to use. Because you will not be meeting any of these people in person at first, your resume needs to represent you. Just as you would want to go to any interview looking professional, you need to make sure that your resume does that for you. Silly errors such as typos can ruin the professional image you are trying so hard to project.

4. **Wrong length.** Your age and life experience usually determine the length of your resume. If you've just graduated from high school, your resume needs to be short. That means one side of one page. You don't make a better impression by including more information.

   If you are older and have been out in the working world for a time, your resume can be longer. However, think carefully before you expand your resume to two pages. Potential training programs or employers may not look beyond the first page.

5. **No active verbs.** Experts advise newbies to include active verbs in their resumes. Active verbs are those parts of speech that indicate actions taking place. Instead of passive verbs such as "is" or "be," use words that tell people what you accomplished or learned in your jobs. "Created new archiving system for documents" sounds better than "was responsible for archiving documents and creation of a new system."

Resume Checklist Worksheet

1st Draft	Description	2nd Draft
	Looks	
☐	Is the resume centered on the page?	☐
☐	Does the resume have enough white space? Does it look as if the writer was stuffing in as much information as the page would allow?	☐
☐	Is the resume font at least 12 pts, so it can be easily read?	☐
☐	Does the resume have sections that are clearly marked?	☐
☐	Does the resume use only one or two font styles throughout?	☐
☐	Is the resume in PDF format so it will look the same on any computer?	☐
	Organization	
☐	Do the section headers make logical sense?	☐
☐	Is the resume the correct length for the career stage of the writer? People with lots of work experience get a longer resume.	☐
☐	Are the past jobs organized with the most recent one first?	☐
☐	Is the resume easy to scan? Can you find the information you want at a glance?	☐
	Content	
☐	Is each full sentence followed by a period?	☐
☐	Does the writer use active verbs to show action in job responsibilities and accomplishments?	☐
☐	Is the writer's past education clearly spelled out?	☐
☐	Does the writer use bullet points to get the main point across quickly?	☐
☐	Has the writer left out all personal information such as age and marital status?	☐
☐	Can you understand from the information provided what the writer did at each job and any accomplishments?	☐

cont.

Resume Checklist Worksheet (cont.)

1st Draft	Description	2nd Draft
	Spelling, Grammar, and Proofreading	
☐	Is the contact information correct, including name, address, phone, and e-mail?	☐
☐	Are there any typos in the document?	☐
☐	Has the writer proofread the document?	☐
☐	Has the writer had someone else proofread the document?	☐
☐	Has the writer used spell-check on the document?	☐

Tracking Resume Versions

Description of Training Program	School or Organization	Title of Resume	Date Sent
Chef school	Johnson & Wales	Chef2011.1.doc	9/23/11

NINE

Interviewing

How to Be Likable

Interviewing for a training opportunity is much the same as interviewing for a job. You need to convince the interviewer that you are the right person for the position—whether the position is a job or an opening in an apprenticeship program. If you are respectful, pay attention to details, and prepare carefully, you can get the position you want. This chapter explains how to prepare in advance, how to dress, and how to behave in order to impress the interviewers.

The key is to be likable. Though it's true that people want to hire people just like themselves, they are also open to working with people they find likable.

Types of Interviews

There are a variety of types of interviews, and it's important that you understand what is required in each one.

Informational Interviews

If you recall, the informational interview was discussed in chapter 1 as a way to find a career you might be interested in. It can also be used to establish a relationship and network with someone in a training program or company you're interested in.

The informational interview is different from any other type of interview. You call to schedule this interview, you do most of the interviewing, and you are the one who benefits the most. Job seekers sometimes use the informational interview (a term first coined by *What Color Is Your Parachute?* author Richard Bolles) to break into a new field or to get inside information from a well-respected expert in the field.

In its most basic form, an informational interview is an interview in which you ask questions of someone who is an expert in a particular field (such as a union member who knows all about the apprenticeship process or an established professional in the field you are interested in entering). You may meet in the expert's office, but you can also invite the expert for coffee (which you will buy) to ask questions.

The idea is to learn everything that the expert can tell you about his or her job. You ask how the expert got involved in the field, about his or her early years in the career, and about anything else the person cares to tell you about, including the responsibilities and duties of the job.

Informational interviews are a great way to build your network while also finding out everything there is to know about a particular job. Job seekers do informational interviews in order to "try on" different jobs to see if a particular job would be a good fit for them. People who are looking for training opportunities can use this type of interview in the same way. You can interview people to find out how the apprenticeship, internship, or other training opportunity works and also to figure out if you would like to do the job after you have completed the apprenticeship or training.

As discussed in chapter 1, informational interviewing is a great option if you don't know exactly what you want to do for a living. You can talk to a wide variety of people in different jobs and get a sense of what you would like to do and what you wouldn't want to do.

On the face of it, it may seem daunting to walk up to strangers and ask them to let you do an interview. Remember, though, that it is quite flattering to have a younger person ask for your career advice. As Dale Carnegie pointed out decades ago, people love to talk about themselves,

Informational Interviewing Basics

Here are some tips to help you ace your informational interview every time:

DON'T ask for a job in an informational interview. People are willing to give you their time because they expect you *not* to do this. (But if someone offers you a job interview, internship, or position at the company, that's fine!)

DO ask for suggestions (or recommendations) about your resume or training.

DON'T let the established professional take control of the conversation. To ensure you cover what you want to discuss, begin the meeting with a brief introduction and explanation of what you'd like to learn during the meeting.

DO ask your interviewee if you can contact him or her again within a couple of weeks to see if he or she has any ideas for your resume or training.

DO take notes. Jot down names of other people to interview or training programs that might be right for you.

and they think very well of people who allow them or even encourage them to do so.

Pretty much everyone in the world (except huge celebrities who are pursued all the time) is flattered to be asked for an informational interview. Many CEOs and other major corporate players are just like the rest of us and cannot resist the urge to pass along their wisdom and insights to the next generation. Try it. You may be surprised at the number of people who are delighted to be asked and can really help you figure out what you want to do.

Start Here

Start by asking people you actually know for an informational interview. This will make you less nervous and help you get experience in the process before you ask total strangers to coffee. You can look at the listings for professional associations for another source of interviewees. The officers of these organizations are often happy to help. You'll want to talk to people who have worked in the job for more than a few years.

Time

You need to keep the interview short. The person is doing you a favor, so stick to 30 to 45 minutes for the first meeting. You can always schedule another interview if you have follow-up questions. You can also send a follow-up e-mail to save time.

Plan in advance what you want to ask. Often it's a good idea to give the other person a heads-up about what you want to know. Your interview subject can take the time to think about your questions, and that helps the interview go more smoothly without wasting time.

Preparation

Be respectful of the other person's time and treat the interview like a job interview. Arrive early. Bring prepared questions with you. Research the person you are interviewing, the company, or the organization so you can ask intelligent questions about the industry. Bring several copies of your resume. Dress nicely and conservatively. Bring a business card to exchange with your expert.

Questions

Take some time to think about what you want to know from the people you interview. Do you want to know about their day-to-day work? Do you want to know their job responsibilities or duties? You can also ask these experts to look at your resume or answer your questions about how to get a job similar to theirs.

Since you're talking about training opportunities and how to get one, feel free to ask your experts how they got into their current job or career. Who did they know? How did they get ahead?

If you're smart, you will also ask your experts about the state of the industry and prospects for the future. After all, you want to think twice about working in an industry that isn't doing well or that will require fewer workers in the future than it does now.

After the interview, send the expert a thank-you note. Be sure to touch on one or more points that you discussed. Thank the expert for his or her time and expertise. You have gained information about the field you want to enter that you can take with you to interviews in which you will be the interviewee: interviews for training programs and jobs.

Telephone Interviews

In the current job market, the telephone interview has become an integral part of the hiring process. It's a way for the hiring manager to screen promising individuals from a large pool of applicants before any are invited to an in-person interview. When you're hunting for training opportunities, you seldom do telephone interviews. Still, if you are competing for a very few spots in a popular training program, you may have to go through a telephone interview before you get asked to attend an in-person interview.

Your goal is to make it through the telephone interview, which is used to weed out unqualified applicants. Even though it's only on the telephone, it is imperative that you take this interview seriously. Research the organization, be prepared with questions to ask, and make sure you turn the telephone interview into a conversation.

Try to mention your job or personal experiences that apply to the training opportunity. Inject some of your personality into the conversation, so the interviewer gets the sense that there's a person behind the voice.

Take notes while you're interviewing so you'll know what the next steps are and what the interviewer is looking for in potential candidates.

In-Person Interviews

The most important step for your in-person interview is to thoroughly research the organization or group that is interviewing you. It also helps to prepare for the interview by doing mock interviews with family and friends.

Work with family and friends in business to help you figure out the questions interviewers may ask. Then practice answering the questions, but don't memorize answers, because you won't sound natural.

Think about the challenges you have faced in your life and how you have overcome them. Interviewers of all types are fond of asking about how you have overcome obstacles. This shows the interviewer how you handle tough situations and approach problems.

Set up practice interviews with friends and make them as similar to a real interview as you can. Wear your suit to make sure you can move in it comfortably. This will help you feel less nervous when you go to the actual interview.

How to Prep for an Interview: Ask a Librarian

If you want to know everything about the organization that is interviewing you or about the union you want to join, ask a librarian. Find the reference librarian at your local library and ask for help. Before you know it, you'll have all the information you need to ace the interview. People who interview candidates like to know that you did your homework and know something about their organization. Your local librarian can help.

Also see if your library offers classes or workshops to help you with job interviews. Even if you are interviewing for a training opportunity, it's the same as a job interview in most respects. Sometimes, your local librarian or another professional is available for mock-interview practice sessions. If this is available at your local library, sign up immediately. Having a really good practice session will help you feel more confident during the real interview.

This preparation will help you feel more confident in your ability to meet new people and answer their questions in a way that helps you win the training opportunities of your dreams.

Follow-up Interviews

Most training opportunities have just one interview. Based on that interview, the organization decides who will get an available spot. Sometimes, though, an organization does follow-up interviews if it has two top candidates for a position.

The follow-up interview is supposed to help the interviewers decide who deserves the opportunity and who will best fit the program. The book *How to Get a Great Job* (American Library Association, 2011) offers excellent advice about how to handle the second and any subsequent interviews:

> Treat all follow-up interviews much like your first interview; don't slack on review of your previous research and repeat your preparation. . . . consider what you didn't get a chance to say, or a point you didn't get a chance to sell, and try to work that into your conversation.
>
> Keep in mind that if you passed the first interview, subsequent meetings may be to see if you are a good fit for the personality or culture of the company, so the questioning may be more personal:

What would you do in this situation? How do you handle conflict? What types of activities do you enjoy in your off-hours?

Group Interviews

Depending on what type of training you are applying for, you may end up with a panel of interviewers all at once instead of just one interviewer at a time. Some companies and organizations do this to save time. They also think that the interviewers will get ideas for follow-up questions from one another. Many organizations also like the idea of one or two interviewers asking questions while one or two more interviewers watch the candidate answer the questions.

Although this kind of interview can be stressful, it is really just a larger conversation that you have to keep going. Instead of speaking to (and looking into the eyes of) one interviewer, you will be making eye contact with the whole panel. The trick to this type of interview is to make it into a group conversation.

Get the other panel members to talk among themselves, and you will be able to find out many things that a single interview with one interviewer couldn't tell you. For example, ask interviewers why they work for the company or what they like best about the company. This is a great question to get your whole panel talking at once and to make the interview into an actual conversation.

What to Say

When people think about going to an interview, most worry about what they will say. Some people feel that it's immodest to talk about themselves and their accomplishments. Others are just nervous about the process and the stress of the situation. The simplest way to get over nervousness is to practice interviewing with friends and family. The more you interview (even just practicing), the better and more relaxed you will be.

First Blood

One goal of your interview should be to get the interviewer to talk. If it works better for you, ask the interviewer to tell you about the training position first. Often it can help you feel less nervous once the interviewer has told you about the opportunity, the process for choosing the right person, and the time line.

Even if the interviewer asks you a question to begin the process, you can ask, "Please, could you tell me more about the position?" Getting the interviewer to talk first is a subtle way to be proactive in the interview. An interview isn't just an opportunity for the interviewer to question you. You also get to ask questions.

Narrative Is Your Friend

Human beings are hard-wired to enjoy stories, and you can use that to your advantage in interviews. Instead of just answering questions, tell a story about how you handled issues in your work or personal life.

A story has a beginning, middle, and end. So start your story with the problem you were dealing with—your challenge. Explain what you did about the challenge—your action. Then detail the results of your action. This method, under several different names, is used frequently these days by human resources people. The advantage of telling a story is that you are also explaining how you would deal with problems or issues during your training or job.

In short, your stories here are a sort of Aesop's fable about how you would deal with problems in your own personal way. Do not underesti-

---

Nonverbal Communication Speaks Loudly

Much of human communication is nonverbal "body language." You may not be fully aware of it, but nonverbal communication has probably played a part in a variety of decisions in your life. For example, did you buy the car from the slippery car salesman who seemed way too perfect? No. Something about the way that person behaved let you know that what he said wasn't true.

Human beings believe more of what they see than of what is said to them. For this reason, you need to be sure that you look good for your interview. Also, make sure your facial expressions and tone of voice agree with what you are saying. If you say that you're excited to be interviewing with the company, make sure you look and sound excited, or the interviewer may not believe you.

mate the power of a good story to show your interviewer why you are the right person for the training opportunity, apprenticeship, internship, or job.

Testing, 1-2-3

Many organizations use some type of test to help assess training candidates. At some point in the interview process, you may be asked to take one, or several. Do your best to find out about any tests beforehand so that you know what you are expected to do during the interview. Here are the most common kinds of tests:

▸ **Assessment test.** These tests are usually multiple-choice. Most of them tell the evaluators about your personality, such as your values, the way you approach problems, and how you get along with others. The test may help them decide if you have the right temperament for their training or organization.

▸ **Skills test.** For some training opportunities, you may be tested on such things as your knowledge of a specific software program, writing skills, or math abilities.

▸ **Typing test.** You may have to take a typing test to show how many words per minute you can type.

▸ **Drug test.** Some programs require drug screening. You may need to pass a drug test as a last step in the admissions or hiring process.

After the Interview

Once the interview is over, you still have a few things to do before you hear the results:

▸ Write down the names and titles of everyone you spoke to during the interview.

▸ If the school or potential employer asked for references, contact those people immediately to notify them that they may soon be hearing from your school or training program. If appropriate, remind them or coach them on what to emphasize about you.

▹ Send a thank-you note to anyone who referred you for the interview, letting them know how it went. This is a good time to thank any informational interviewees who may have put in a good word for you with the admissions or hiring committee.

▹ Send thank-you notes to your interviewers. Sending a prompt, succinct, and well-written thank-you note to each person you interviewed with is a crucial step. Why? Because it is one more opportunity for you to make an impression and stand out from your competition, to sell your best qualifications, and to prove you are an excellent match for the training opportunity.

If you asked—and were told—that the admission, scholarship, or hiring decision would be made within two weeks, contact the school or employer a couple of days before that estimated deadline. If you don't know the time frame, wait about a week after the interview before making contact, and then call or e-mail the person you interviewed with to say thank you again and to restate your interest in admission or the position you applied for. You can leave this information in a voicemail message, but call only once to leave your message.

If you still don't hear back after your first follow-up e-mail or voice-mail, try again a week later. If you don't get a reply to your second message, you are probably no longer in the running for admittance, the scholarship, or the position. If you get to the interview stage, it is proper etiquette for the interviewer to let you know by phone or e-mail what the decision is, whether you got the opportunity or not. But, unfortunately, some interviewers lack good etiquette, and some human resources departments are not very organized. As disheartening as it can be to get no response, it happens to everyone, and it is time to move on to the next opportunity at this point.

If you get bad news, write your main contact with the organization a gracious e-mail, letting that person know that you are disappointed but still interested in the organization and in the field. Tell him or her that you would appreciate being kept in mind for future opportunities should any open up. Later you may want to apply at this company or for this program again, and you want to end this experience on a positive note. Keep in mind, also, that your behavior reflects on any person or people who may have referred you to this job or training opportunity.

Interview Toolbox:
Interview Tips for Your Appearance

Here are five great tips to make sure you look and feel great for your interview:

1. *Use mints.* No matter what you had for lunch, remember to bring mints with you and eat them about ten minutes before your interview. You don't want bad breath to ruin your interview. You can also chew gum, but remember to throw it away before the interview.

2. *Skip the perfume or cologne.* Many people are allergic to intense smells such as perfume or cologne. Even if your interviewer isn't allergic, you don't want to wear scent when you will be sitting in a small room. Strong scents can annoy interviewers or cause them to be sick. That means aftershave, too, for men.

3. *Don't be too revealing.* Sexy, low-cut tops or skin-tight clothes may be perfect for wearing to a club or out on a date, but they can be distracting in a job interview. Your interviewer could be distracted and not pay attention to anything but your cleavage or could be put off by your revealing display. Go for conservative clothes in darker, muted colors.

4. *Check your suit for repairs.* Most people do not wear their interview suit every day. For this reason, you may not be aware that your suit is missing a button, that your blouse has a tear, or that your tie has a stain. A week or so before your interview, check out your interview wear to make sure everything is pressed, clean, and looking good. You don't want to find out that your pants have a rip when you're sitting in the waiting room before your interview.

5. *Shine your shoes.* It sounds old-fashioned, but you need to shine your shoes before you go to an interview. If your shoes aren't the right material for shining, then brush them or otherwise make sure they are clean, free of mud or dirt, and good-looking. This tip applies to women as well as men.

Bonus tip: When in doubt, dress up. Training programs and schools can be pretty casual places, but that doesn't mean that the admission committee expects you to wear jeans and sneakers to your interview.

Thank-You Note Know-How

Write a separate (and unique) note to every person you interviewed with.

Send your notes within 24 to 48 hours of the interview.

It's often acceptable to e-mail a thank-you note, but writing or typing one and mailing it is better. A handwritten note is best of all.

Send a thank-you note even if the interview did not go well or if you know you are no longer in the running for admission. Thank the interviewers for their time and consideration.

Keep it brief: state your thanks, one highlight of your accomplishments or one reference to a point that came up during the interview, and your interest in being admitted to the school or training program—or being hired for the job.

You'd be surprised how many times a gracious response to a "rejection" actually works out well for a job applicant in the long run; your contact at the company may have had many reasons having nothing to do with you for not giving you the job. You may have been his or her personal favorite candidate, and your professional reaction will be impressive enough to get you a call later for a job opportunity more suited to you. Likewise, an opening may come up in the training program you applied for. You are at the top of the waiting list for that spot if you treat people at the organization with respect and professionalism, even when you get bad news.

Interview Checklist

Research

- ☐ Look the organization up on the Internet.
- ☐ Ask your local reference librarian to help you find more information about the organization.

Appearance

- ☐ Get suit cleaned.
- ☐ Polish or brush shoes.
- ☐ Get clean socks or hose.
- ☐ Find briefcase or portfolio to bring to interview.
- ☐ Choose jewelry for interview. (Remember, less is more.)

Preparation

- ☐ Write a list of questions to ask during the interview.
- ☐ How will you get to the interview? Where will you park? Do you need driving directions? Do you have the address?
- ☐ Do you need to bring ID to get into the building where you are interviewing?
- ☐ Do you have paper and pens to take notes during the interview?
- ☐ Do you know the name of your interviewer?
- ☐ Do you have three or four copies of your resume with you? (You will need more than one in case you are in a panel interview or meet more than one person.)
- ☐ Do you have one or two copies of your list of references?
- ☐ Will they ask you to take a test during the interview?

Miscellaneous

- ☐ Have you asked the interviewer about dress code?
- ☐ Have you asked the interviewer who you will meet or what to bring?

Aftermath

- ☐ Did you get business cards from every person you interviewed with?
- ☐ Send snail-mail or e-mail thank-you notes to everyone you interviewed with.

Interview Tracking Sheet

	Organization 1	Organization 2	Organization 3
Date application sent			
Interview date			
Interview time			
Interview address including suite number			
Ask for driving directions?			
How long will interview take?			
Taking a test during interview? What type?			
How many interviewers?			
Name of main interviewer			
Names of other interviewers			

TEN

Paying for Training and Education

Estimating Costs and Applying for Financial Aid

One of the most important choices you will make in your life is deciding how to pay for your training and education after high school. This chapter can help you figure out how much it will cost and find ways to pay for it, including financial aid. Some people think that financial aid is only for people who attend four-year colleges and universities. Nothing could be further from the truth. The same types of financial aid are usually available for community colleges, vocational and technical schools, and online classes.

Before you begin applying for financial aid, you need to figure out two things: how much your training program or school will cost and what personal resources you have to pay for it.

Costs

Total training costs generally fall into one of the following five categories.

Program Costs and Fees

These costs are the easiest to estimate, since most training programs and schools list them on their websites. Some list costs, sometimes referred to as tuition, per credit hour, but many figure costs based on how many classes you take.

Residence

If you will be living away from home, the training program may have residence halls where you can live and eat, or you may have to find your own place to live. If your training program doesn't have residence halls, you will need to pay the rent on an apartment or a room. If you are living with your parents, you may or may not have many expenses in this category.

Books and Supplies

The costs for books and supplies can vary greatly, depending on your training program. If you're going to cooking school, for example, your supplies may include a chef's uniform to wear and a very pricey knife kit. So be sure to find out the cost of supplies when you check out the website for your training program.

Travel

If you live close to your training program or will be taking courses online, the travel costs will be minimal. If you will be taking courses online, the college or training program may still require that you take one or two trips a year to the campus for on-site classes. If so, you will probably be offered low-cost housing to stay in during your visit. Check with your online program coordinator to determine whether you will need to travel to the campus and the average cost of these trips. If you will be living on campus, make sure to include the costs of returning home for school breaks and over the summer, if appropriate.

Personal Expenses

Personal expenses such as laundry, cell phone, entertainment, and meals can really add up, and they are one area where your behavior can make a huge difference in your budget. When you're paying for a training program or other education, you might have to cut back on some of the less basic expenses.

If you have no idea how to estimate some of these costs, visit the College Affordability and Transparency Center website, sponsored by the Department of Education, and click on "How much do career and vocational programs cost?" on the main page, http://collegecost.ed.gov/catc. You can enter the program you wish to attend, click Go, and the site will give you a detailed report of current tuition and fees for that program, average costs of book and supplies, and average living expenses for students living on campus, off campus, and off campus with parents. College Navigator, http://nces.ed.gov/collegenavigator, is a user-friendly website that also provides detailed estimates of most costs associated with each program.

Personal Resources

There are generally two kinds of personal resources: your parents' and your own. Some parents pay for their children's training programs or provide some financial assistance. Before asking your parents to pay for anything, make sure they examine their finances, consult an accountant, and check with the financial aid office of your training program so that they (and you) understand the full range of tax and financial aid advantages and disadvantages.

Following are some ways that parents can help pay for their children's training programs.

529 Savings Plans

Named for a section of the IRS code that created them, 529 savings plans (or 529 plans, as they are usually called) were created specifically to help parents, grandparents, and other family members save for education. There are two types of 529 plans: prepaid tuition plans and college savings plans. It is difficult to generalize about these plans because they are run by each individual state, and each state can offer different options and tax advantages. For more details about 529 plans, visit the website for the College Savings Plan Network, www.collegesavings.org. If you choose to invest in one of these plans, it is a good idea to get the advice of a financial planner to choose the best one for your needs. Start early. If the account won't start accruing funds when the student is in high school, it's probably not worthwhile to start investing in a 529 plan, although some online education "gift registries" (discussed later in this chapter) require users to have a 529 savings plan.

Coverdell Education Savings Accounts

Coverdell accounts were created as an incentive to help parents and students save for education expenses. Contributions grow tax-free until the benefits are distributed. The total contributions for the beneficiary on this account can't exceed $2,000 in any year, and the beneficiary must be under 18 when the account is established. The beneficiary will not owe taxes on the distributions if they are less than the beneficiary's qualified education expenses at an eligible institution. Education tax credits can be claimed in the same year the beneficiary takes a tax-free distribution from a Coverdell account as long as the same expenses are not used for both benefits. Read more about Coverdell ESAs on the IRS website at www .irs.gov/publications/p970/ch07.html.

Social Networking Savings Programs, Credit Card Rebates, and Loyalty Programs

A variety of companies offer incentive plans that allow friends, family, and even casual acquaintances of students to help them save for college. Think of them as a bridal registry for college students.

Only a few such programs have managed to stay in business during the economic downturn, including GradSave (www.gradsave.com) and GradeFund (www.gradefund.com). To protect students from online preda-tors, a student's information can be restricted so that it is visible to only those people the student already knows.

Loyalty or affinity programs have been around for a long time, but they have only recently been used to help fund college education. You register your credit and debit cards with a company. When you use your cards to buy certain products or buy from certain stores, a rebate is sent to the college fund of your choice. Upromise (www.upromise.com) has one of the biggest networks of retailers, and it was recently purchased by student loan giant Sallie Mae. As of 2007, you can even earmark your rebates to pay off the student loan balances of those you love.

Savings Bonds

U.S. savings bonds have been the go-to graduation gift for many years, and the Series EE and Series I bonds can be used to pay for college. The Education Savings Bond Program makes these bonds tax-free when they are used to pay for college expenses or rolled over into a 529 savings plan.

Education Tax Credits and Deductions

A variety of education tax credits can also help you or your parents pay for your training. Only one of these credits may be claimed in one tax year per student.

The *Lifetime Learning Credit* is available for all years of postsecondary education and for courses to acquire or improve job skills. The qualifying student does not need to be pursuing a degree or other recognized education credential. Eligible expenses are tuition and fees required for enrollment or attendance, including money required to be paid to the learning institution for course-related books, supplies, and equipment. The maximum credit per year is $2,000.

The new *American Opportunity Tax Credit*, introduced in 2009 and extended through 2012, targets low- and middle-income students. It can be claimed for expenses paid for tuition, certain fees, and course materials. Unlike the Lifetime Learning Credit, this tax credit includes expenses for course-related books, supplies, and equipment that are not paid to the learning institution. The maximum annual credit is $2,500. Up to $1,000 of this credit is refundable, meaning you can get it even if you owe no tax. Congress is debating whether this tax credit will be extended beyond 2012. Check the IRS website, www.irs.gov, for updates.

There are income limitations for both credits. Should you not qualify for either of those options, you may be able to take deductions on eligible expenses. For an overview of available tax benefits for education, see http://studentaid.ed.gov/types/tax-benefits.

Parents must keep meticulous records when using these bonds, including recording the educational institution, the date each qualified educational expense was paid, and the amount of the expense as well as the bond serial number, the face value, the date issued, the date redeemed, and the total amount of the bond at maturity. For more information, visit Treasury Direct's "Education Planning" web page, www.treasurydirect .gov/indiv/planning/plan_education.htm.

Individual Retirement Accounts and 401(k) Plans

While it is possible in most cases to withdraw funds from retirement plans for a qualified higher education expense or a training program for yourself, your spouse, your child, or your grandchild without paying a penalty for early withdrawal, many financial planners discourage it. A federal PLUS loan, discussed later in this chapter, is currently a better deal for most people.

Home Equity Line of Credit

One main advantage of using a home equity line of credit to pay for training programs is that the market value of your house (your *primary residence* in IRS-speak) is usually not taken into account by the federal financial aid formulas. This used to be a popular way to pay for school, but it is also what helped a lot of people get into trouble during the recent housing crash. At a time when so many homeowners are underwater on their mortgages, this may not be a good idea. Again, the federal PLUS loan discussed later in this chapter is a better deal right now for most people.

Finding and Applying for Financial Aid

Many people are surprised that they can receive financial aid for a certificate program or two-year degree. In reality, they can receive most of the same kinds of financial aid as four-year-degree seekers. Visit the financial aid office of the trade school or technical, vocational, or community college you're considering to ensure that the degree or certificate program you'd like to enroll in meets financial aid eligibility. Not all schools participate in the federal student aid program. Federal student aid from the U.S. Department of Education is the largest source of student aid in

America—each year, it awards about $150 billion in grants, work-study, and federal loans to more than 14 million students attending colleges, universities, community colleges, and career schools. When you are selecting your program, you will want to make sure you have financial aid options.

Financial aid comes in many forms. Grants, scholarships, and federal low-interest loans are the most popular. Grants are funds primarily awarded based on need, and they do not need to be paid back. Scholarships are funds awarded for academic achievement, religious affiliation, skills, ethnic background, or a variety of other characteristics of the recipient, and they also don't have to be paid back. Federal loans are money that is borrowed from the U.S. government at special low rates. All loans have to be repaid with interest.

There are more forms of financial aid described later in this chapter, but you will always start your financial aid search by filling out one form: the FAFSA.

The FAFSA

For most students, applying for financial aid means filling out the Free Application for Federal Student Aid (FAFSA) (pronounced FAHF-suh). You must complete the FAFSA to apply for federal student financial aid and most other state and college aid. To be eligible for federal student aid, you must meet the following basic requirements:

▸ Be a U.S. citizen or eligible noncitizen
▸ Have a valid Social Security number
▸ Register with Selective Service, if required
▸ Have a high school diploma or GED (there are some exceptions)
▸ Be enrolled or accepted for enrollment as a student working toward a degree, certificate, or other recognized credential in an eligible program at a school that participates in the federal student aid program

Many training programs, colleges, and universities use the FAFSA to figure out the financial aid they will give their students. In the online FAFSA form, at www.fafsa.ed.gov, you can list up to ten schools or training programs that you want your FAFSA information sent to. There's an online directory, so you can search for the name of each program or school. Filling out the FAFSA online rather than on paper saves you about fourteen days in the application process, especially if you sign the online form with a PIN. You will probably want to request the PIN, at www.pin .ed.gov, before you start filling out the FAFSA.

The FAFSA is a long, complex form that asks for a lot of personal and financial information. If you need help filling it out, visit www.fafsa.ed .gov and click on "Help" at the top of the page. The Help page also lists many ways to get assistance. If the Help database doesn't answer your questions you can chat live through a secure online session with a customer service representative or call 1-800-4-FED-AID (1-800-433-3243). TTY users can call 1-800-730-8913.

Within a few days of submitting your FAFSA electronically, you will receive your Student Aid Report (SAR), which details your Expected Family Contribution (EFC), the amount the government believes your family can contribute to your education expenses. It is important that you look your SAR over for any errors because this is what your institution will use to determine how much financial aid you need. Eventually, you will receive financial aid award letters from all schools where you have been accepted and from which you requested financial aid. Award letters tell you exactly how much financial support the school is able to provide for the upcoming year. It is important to know that you may decline any portion of the aid, for example, if you decide you don't need a work-study position or a federal loan.

Check with the financial aid office for each school or program for its FAFSA deadline. Make sure to submit your FAFSA before the deadline and remember to reapply each year you are in school to stay eligible for aid.

Grants

Grants are often awarded based on financial need and do not have to be repaid. According to the College Board, the 31 percent of all U.S. undergraduate students enrolled in two-year colleges received 32 percent of the total Pell Grant funds in the 2009–10 school year. Grants are offered by your state, the federal government, and other institutions, such as schools and employers.

There are three types of federal grants available to you. In order to be considered for these, all you need to do is submit the FAFSA. And remember, you will have to reapply every year.

Pell Grant

Pell Grants are awarded to students based on need. To receive a Pell Grant, you must be an undergraduate or vocational student who does not have a bachelor's or a professional degree. The maximum annual award for 2012–2013 is $5,550, but the amount is subject to change each year. If you are eligible for a Pell Grant and your parent or guardian was a member of the U.S. armed forces and died as a result of military service in Iraq or Afghanistan after the events of September 11, 2001, you may be eligible for additional Pell funds. For more information on Pell Grants, visit http://studentaid.ed.gov/types/grants-scholarships/pell.

Federal Supplemental Educational Opportunity Grant (FSEOG)

In order to receive this grant, you must be eligible for a Pell Grant and have exceptional financial need. The maximum annual award for 2012–

Military Student Aid

The Montgomery GI Bill, which helps people who have served in the military afford to pay for education, is the reason some people enlist in the armed forces. However, the GI Bill benefits cover only a portion of the costs of college. Here are some more options for you if you've served your country or are a dependent of someone in the armed forces:

Scholarships for Military Children: www.militaryscholar.org

Iraq and Afghanistan Service Grant: http://studentaid.ed.gov/types/grants-scholarships/iraq-afghanistan-service

Scholarships for Military Families and Military Service: www.studentaid.ed.gov/military

The Post-9/11 GI Bill: www.gibill.va.gov/benefits/post_911_gibill

Survivors & Dependents Assistance (DEA): www.gibill.va.gov/benefits/other_programs/dea.html

Veterans Educational Assistance Program (VEAP): www.gibill.va.gov/benefits/other_programs/veap.html

Reserve Educational Assistance Program (REAP): www.gibill.va.gov/benefits/other_programs/reap.html

Additional Pell Grant funds: http://studentaid.ed.gov/types/grants-scholarships/pell

Veterans Retraining Assistance Program (VRAP): http://benefits.va.gov/vow/education.htm

---

Deadline Alert: Financial Aid Deadlines

You and your parents should fill out the FAFSA starting on January 1 every year. Financial aid advisors suggest that you and your parents get your taxes done *before* January 1 so that you can fill out the FAFSA online in the early days of January. It's also a good idea to check in with your financial aid office to double-check any deadlines particular to the financial aid your school offers.

2013 is $4,000. For more information, visit http://studentaid.ed.gov/types/grants-scholarships/FSEOG.

Iraq and Afghanistan Service Grant

This grant is for students not eligible for a Pell Grant (only because of that program's need requirements) and whose parent or guardian died as a result of military service in Iraq or Afghanistan after the events of September 11, 2001. You must have been under 24 or enrolled in college at the time of your parent or guardian's death. The maximum award is always the same as the maximum for the Pell Grant in any given year, but the award can't exceed the cost of attendance of a school or training program for that award year. For more information, visit http://studentaid.ed.gov/types/grants-scholarships/iraq-afghanistan-service.

Nonfederal Grants

Some schools provide institutional grants to help with expenses that cannot be met through income, savings, loans, and student earnings. Contact the financial aid office at the community college, trade school, or vocational college you're applying to and inquire about institutional or merit grants. These types of grants will usually have to be applied for individually, and the tips for applying for scholarships, in the next section, will help you with these kinds of grant applications.

You will also want to check with the department of labor for your state. Each state has different scholarship, grant, and loan programs. Grant agencies for all states, including their websites, are listed here: http://wdcrobcolp01.ed.gov/programs/erod/org_list.cfm?category_cd=sgt. Some states have separate funds to train workers in high-demand occupations.

If you are holding a job while you are training, ask your employer if it offers a tuition reimbursement grant as part of your benefits. Quite a few employers reimburse employees for a portion of their tuition expenses if the education or training is job-related.

Scholarships

Scholarships, like grants, do not have to be repaid. Although nearly every college student wants a scholarship, only about half of all college students are expected to receive any free money in the next few years. Because of the downturn in the economy, many schools are slashing their scholarship programs, and this trend is expected to continue. Many states are also cutting their scholarship programs. To make matters worse, because of the high demand for scholarships, many financial aid programs are setting higher grade, test score, and other requirements.

That said, every single unique fact about you could represent a scholarship opportunity. Think African American air traffic controller from upstate New York, or daughter of a Filipino soldier applying to an electrician apprenticeship program, or police officer whose ancestors came

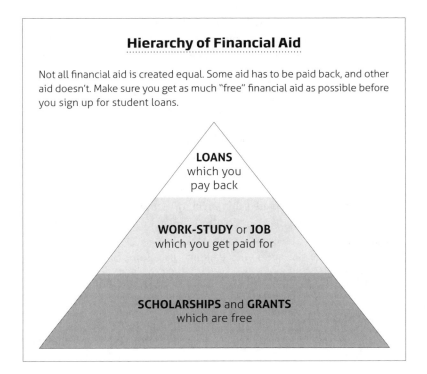

Hierarchy of Financial Aid

Not all financial aid is created equal. Some aid has to be paid back, and other aid doesn't. Make sure you get as much "free" financial aid as possible before you sign up for student loans.

LOANS
which you
pay back

WORK-STUDY or **JOB**
which you get paid for

SCHOLARSHIPS and **GRANTS**
which are free

over on the *Mayflower*. It's the combination of these things that makes you scholarship-worthy.

There are scholarships for people with an interesting ethnic background, those who are going into specific careers, and even those who hail from a particular state or region of the country.

> ▷ **Take a personal inventory.** Start by filling out the Personal Inventory form at the end of this chapter. Answering all of the questions ensures that you have left no stone unturned in seeking free money for school.
> ▷ **Include your relatives.** Checking out the jobs, careers, professional organizations, volunteer activities, and hobbies of your parents, grandparents, and other relatives can yield big rewards in the scholarship category. Many corporations have in-house foundations that give scholarships to the children and grandchildren of employees. In addition, most professional organizations (e.g., International Association of Engineers, Association of Realtors) also give scholarships in their fields.
> ▷ **Consider your out-of-school activities.** Some scholarships are more interested in your out-of-school activities than in your schoolwork because they value a well-rounded individual and put their scholarship money where their beliefs are.
> ▷ **Share information about yourself.** Although some of the questions on the Personal Inventory form are personal (especially those about your sexual preference and religious beliefs), there are groups out there that give scholarships based on these traits. Answering the questions can help you find scholarships that many of your classmates may not be qualified to apply for.

Once you have completed this inventory, move on to the following section that tells you where to look for scholarships. Several scholarship websites allow you to search by keyword or browse available scholarships by type. The information in your Personal Inventory form will give you some keywords and themes to search by and look for.

Where to Look for Scholarships

Look both online and offline for scholarship opportunities.

Online scholarship searches are easy and effective as long as you remember to fill in search forms completely. Here's a list of free scholarship search sites:

College Board Scholarship Search: https://bigfuture.collegeboard
.org/scholarship-search

College View Scholarships, Financial Aid, and Grants: www.college
view.com/financialaid/salliemae.jsp

CollegeNet.com Scholarships Search: www.collegenet.com/
mach25/app

Fastweb Scholarships: www.fastweb.com/college-scholarships

Military.com Scholarship Finder: http://aid.military.com/scholar
ship/search-for-scholarships.do

Sallie Mae's Scholarship Search: http://go.salliemae.com/scholar
ship

Scholarships.com: www.scholarships.com

U.S. Department of Labor Scholarship Search: www.careerinfonet
.org/scholarshipsearch

If you are looking for scholarships, you may have to do some "old school" research, with books. But you don't have to go it alone. Ask reference librarians and high school counselors for their help. Here are a couple of good books to consider:

> ▸ *The Ultimate Scholarship Book 2013* (published every year).
> Gen and Kelly Tanabe have written an excellent resource for
> anyone looking for scholarships. Their listing of scholarships is
> good, but their advice about finding and pursuing scholarships
> is brilliant. From personal experience, they tell you exactly how
> to position yourself to win. If you can't afford this book, borrow
> it from your local library.
> ▸ *The Scholarship Handbook 2013* (published every year). The
> College Board has put together a really useful tool to find the
> right scholarships for you. There are 1.7 million students who
> win scholarship awards every year, and you can be one of them.

Networking is what most people do to get a job these days, but it also works as a method to find scholarships. You are only one person. If you ask everyone you know and they ask everyone they know, soon you will be awash in scholarship information. Be sure and ask your high school counselor and the financial aid office at the school you plan to attend.

And don't forget about social media. If you put the word out on Facebook or Twitter that you want to know about scholarships, you'll be putting the best of the "old school" and the "new school" together for your own benefit.

How to Apply for Scholarships

Most scholarships require at least an application form. Many require high school transcripts, letters of recommendation, and an essay from you. Be sure to check each scholarship and grant website carefully to see what it requires and when you have to submit it.

Scholarship-granting organizations will not consider applications that come in late. Few scholarships require a personal interview, but you need to be prepared in case you are a finalist for one of those that does. You should not have to pay a fee to apply for a scholarship. If fees are required, you may want to look more closely at the scholarship to see if it's a scam. (Visit http://studentair.ed.gov/types/scams to learn how to spot scholarship scams.)

Here are some great websites to help you win scholarships:

College Board, How to Apply for a Scholarship: https://bigfuture
.collegeboard.org/pay-for-college/scholarships-and-grants/
how-to-apply-for-a-college-scholarship
College Answer Scholarship Application Tips: www.college
answer.com/paying-for-college/free-money-for-college/college
-scholarships/scholarship-application-tips.aspx
Scholarships.com: www.scholarships.com/financial-aid/college
-scholarships/scholarship-application-strategies

Work-Study

The federal work-study program (FWS) provides part-time jobs for undergraduate and graduate students with financial need, allowing them to earn money to help pay education expenses. The program encourages community service work and work related to the recipient's course of study. This money is given to the school and is finite. If you are interested in a work-study position, submit your FAFSA early and indicate that you would like to be considered for the work-study program.

Loans

Loans are debts that you have to pay back, with interest. Loans can be a helpful way to pay for college and training. But consider this: Over the last decade, student debt has nearly tripled to a staggering $1 trillion. More and more students are struggling to repay their loans. And unlike other kinds of debt, it is almost impossible to make student loans go away when you declare bankruptcy. So think very carefully before you take out a loan.

Federal Loans

There are three types of federal student loans. Each type of loan has different conditions, including interest rates, repayment options, and who may borrow the money. To apply for the first two kinds of loans, all you have to do is fill out the FAFSA.

Perkins Loans

Perkins loans are low-interest loans offered to full- or part-time students with exceptional need. If you qualify for a Perkins loan, it is almost always a good idea to take it. Your school is the lender, and the loan is made with government funds. You must repay this loan to your school. You can borrow up to $5,500 for each year of undergraduate study, and the current interest rate is 5 percent. There are no fees for this kind of loan, but if you skip a payment, pay late, or make less than a full payment, you might have to pay a late charge plus any collection charges. If you're attending at least half-time, you have nine months after you graduate, leave school, or drop below half-time status before you must begin repayment. For more information, visit http://studentaid.ed.gov/types/loans/perkins.

Direct Loans

Direct loans are low-interest loans for eligible recipients who are at least half-time students to help cover the cost of education at a college or university, community college, or trade, career, or technical school. Eligible students borrow directly from the U.S. Department of Education at participating schools. Direct loans can be subsidized (the government pays the interest while the student is in training during the grace period, and during deferment periods) or unsubsidized (interest is charged as soon as the loan

---

Help for Student Borrowers

In 2007, Congress passed the College Cost Reduction and Access Act, which created two new federal programs to help people handle their student loan debt: a new Public Service Loan Forgiveness program and a new Income-Based Repayment plan (IBR) for the repayment of federal loans.

The Public Service Loan Forgiveness Program offers forgiveness for outstanding Federal Direct loans for those individuals who make 120 qualifying payments while working full-time in a "public service job," which includes federal, state, and local government jobs as well as many in the non-profit sector. For more information, visit www.studentaid.ed.gov/publicservice.

The new Income-Based Repayment plan helps to make repaying major federal education loans more affordable for low-income borrowers. For more information, visit www.ibrinfo.org.

---

is disbursed). Currently, the interest rate for subsidized Direct loans is 3.4 percent; the interest rate for unsubsidized Direct loans is 6.8 percent.

One of the great features of Direct loans is that students who have taken them out can sign up for income-based repayment when they leave school, so that their monthly student loan bills won't bust their budgets if they don't get high-paying jobs right away. The amount of the loan varies, depending your classification (dependent versus independent undergraduate). There is a processing fee of 1 percent of the amount of the loan. You have a six-month grace period after graduation or dropping below half-time enrollment to begin repayment. For more information on Direct loans, visit www.direct.ed.gov.

Direct PLUS

There are two types of Direct PLUS loans. Only one of these, the Direct PLUS loan for parents, is for undergraduates. Biological or adoptive parents, or stepparents, in some cases, of dependent students may apply for a Direct PLUS loan to help pay for a child's education expenses.

Unlike with the Direct and Perkins loans, you can be turned down for a Direct PLUS loan based on your credit score. The annual limit is equal to the student's cost of attendance minus any other financial aid the student receives. Currently, the interest rate is fixed at 7.9 percent. Interest is charged from the date of the first disbursement until the loan is paid in full. There is a fee of 4 percent, deducted proportionally at the time of each disbursement. The grace period on this loan is six months. It is not eligible for income-based repayment.

Private Loans

Because the interest rates are so much better than what people can qualify for from private sources, most financial aid experts advise students and their families to exhaust federal loans before resorting to private loans. Federal loans offer benefits not typically offered by private lenders, such as low, fixed interest rates, income-based repayment plans, and deferment options. Private loans can come from your local bank, your state, your college or college foundation, and even organizations such as the aid societies for the U.S. military branches. The major private-loan providers, including Sallie Mae and Wells Fargo & Co., now offer fixed-rate student loans, which are an improvement over variable-rate loans. Some private lenders are offering rates that are lower than federal Direct PLUS loans, some as low as 5 percent. However, parents' credit scores must be very high for them to get these kinds of rates.

Be careful about taking out a loan to pay for your training program. You have to pay loans back with interest. Be a smart loan consumer by following these tips:

> ▶ **Compare rates and shop around.** Compare the interest rate, the repayment schedule, and the other terms of the loan.
> ▶ **Take only what you need.** Borrow only what you think you will need for one year of training. You can always go back and borrow more if you need it.
> ▶ **Ask about fees.** Ask to have the fees explained, so you know what they are for.

Tax Deductions for Your Student Loan

Parents can deduct the interest payments on loans they take out for the education of their children on their taxes. Students who take out loans for their own education can take the same deduction. Read IRS Publication 970 (Tax Benefits for Education) at www.irs.gov/publications/p970 for more details.

Finding a Private Loan

If you have to take out a private loan, there are a variety of places you can look, including the bank. If you have a checking and savings account at a bank or credit union, it may be willing to lend you money for college. Go in and check with a banking executive. If your parents have a small business or have been doing business with the same bank or credit union for years, you may want to talk with that bank manager or another executive about a student loan.

> The College Board includes student loans in its scholarship search engine: https://bigfuture.collegeboard.org/scholarship-search
>
> Military.com has a listing of scholarships, grants, and loans for those in the military community, including veterans, spouses, and children of soldiers: http://aid.military.com/scholarship/search-for-scholarships.do
>
> Sallie Mae offers student loans along with 529 savings plans: www.salliemae.com

When you start looking at loans, make sure you understand the specialized terminology. A glossary of financial aid and loan terms is included below. A more complete glossary can be found at http://studentaid.ed.gov/glossary.

A Glossary of Financial Aid Terms

Cancellation: This is when a bank cancels a loan.

Capitalizing the loan: This means that you add the yearly interest to the principal of a loan.

Credit check: Some loans from the federal government don't do credit checks. They are based on the student applicant's needs and are backed by the government. Other federal loans and all private loans do check credit history.

Data Release Number (DRN): FAFSA assigns this number to your application. You need the DRN to change your mailing address or to have your SAR sent to additional schools.

Deferment: The bank allows you to put your monthly loan payments on hold.

Disbursement: The loan check your financial aid office gives you once or twice a year.

Expected Family Contribution (EFC): The amount FAFSA believes your family can contribute to your college costs. It is listed in the SAR.

FAFSA: Free Application for Federal Student Aid.

FAFSA transaction number: When you submit your FAFSA or make a correction to it, a transaction number is created.

Federal methodology: This is the formula FAFSA uses to figure out your family's EFC on your SAR.

Financial need: This is what the financial aid office at your school figures out based on your SAR and the cost of attending that school.

Forbearance: The bank allows you to stop making monthly loan payments for a short time because you are having financial difficulties.

Grant: Most grants are awarded based on need. Grants don't have to be repaid. They are awarded by your state, the federal government, and other institutions.

Interest rate: This is how much you will be paying every year for the privilege of borrowing money (loans).

Loan consolidation: The bank puts all of your student loans together into one bigger loan.

Needs assessment: This is the FAFSA and any other financial aid form that indicates how much money you will need to attend your training program.

Needs-based: The loan is based on the financial need of the student as determined by FAFSA.

PIN: This is a four-digit number you can use to sign your FAFSA electronically and to view your SAR or correct information on your FAFSA.

Repayment schedule: Most federal student loans are meant to be paid back within ten years of finishing your training program.

Scholarship: Scholarships are awarded based on certain characteristics of the applicant, including special skills or talents, academic achievement, religious affiliation, and ethnic background, and they don't have to be repaid.

Signature page: This page is required by FAFSA. You can use an electronic signature (a PIN) to sign it online or print out and sign a paper form.

Student Aid Report (SAR): The SAR is the report that tells you, your parents, and your school how much your parents can afford to pay (the EFC).

Subsidized: The federal government pays the interest rate on the student loan until the student graduates from college or is not enrolled at least half-time as a student.

Work-study: This is a federal program at schools that allows students to work during the school year and be paid from financial aid money.

Scholarship or Grant Personal Inventory

Personal Characteristic

Ancestry

Country where parents were born	
County where grandparents were born	
Ethnicity: Arab, black, Native American, etc.	
Ancestors came over on the *Mayflower*? (Daughters of the American Revolution)	
Ancestors fought in the Civil War? (Daughters of the Confederacy)	
Female?	
Adopted?	
In foster care?	
Racial minority?	
Mixed race?	

Religious Affiliation

Of parents?	
Of grandparents?	
Of student?	

Financial Need (based on FAFSA data)

Expected Family Contribution? (EFC)	
Recent financial issues (job loss, foreclosure)?	
Student independent of parents?	

cont.

Personal Characteristic

Parents and Grandparents

Jobs	
In politics?	
In military?	
Own small business?	
Work for company with a foundation?	
Belong to a professional organization (ABA, Engineering Association)?	
Work in public service occupation (social worker, teacher, lawyer for low-income clients)?	
Doctors, lawyers, veterinarians, or teachers?	
Work for a union?	
Own a farm?	
Police or firefighters?	
Work for federal government?	
Work for state government?	
Volunteer in the community?	
Members of fraternal organizations?	
Serve on the board of not-for-profit organizations?	
Political affiliations?	

Personal Characteristic

Student Information: School

GPA	
GPA in subject of training program	
Extracurricular activities	
Team sports	
Non-team sports	
Arts activities	

Student Information: Outside School

Volunteer activities	
Hobbies	
Membership in civic organizations	

Student Information: Jobs

Employer has foundation (e.g., McDonald's, OfficeMax)	
Previous employer had foundation	

Student Information: Personal

Sexual preference	
Physical impairment	
Learning disability	
Political affiliation	
Religious affiliation	
Athletics outside school	
Music, dance outside school	

cont.

Scholarship or Grant Personal Inventory (cont.)

Personal Characteristic

Writing outside school	
Crafts, skills outside school	
Career goal (can be tentative)	

Student Information: Training Programs

Programs applied to	
Program has foundation that gives scholarships?	

Location Information

State	
County	
City	
Local major league sports teams (often have foundations)	
Local civic organizations	
Local teachers union	
High school booster club	
High school alumni group	
PTA or parents' organization for high school	
Local state representative	
Local member of congress	
Local newspaper	
Local television station	
Local radio station	

Training and Education Resources Worksheet

Parents

529 savings plan	
Coverdell Education Savings Account	
Affinity or loyalty programs	
Savings bonds	
Savings plans in parents' names	
Tax credit: American Opportunity	
Tax credit: Lifetime Learning	
Tax deduction: eligible education expenses	

Student

Affinity or loyalty programs	
Student savings account	
Savings bonds	
Graduation gifts from family and friends	
Social networking savings plans	

Resources

Application Essays

Books

Gelb, Alan. *Conquering the College Admissions Essay in 10 Steps: Crafting a Winning Personal Statement*. Berkeley, CA: Ten Speed Press, 2008.

McGinty, Sarah Myers. *The College Application Essay*, 5th ed. New York: College Board, 2012.

Websites

About.com: College Admissions
http://collegeapps.about.com/od/theartofgettingaccepted/u/The_Application.htm#s4
Read sample personal, supplemental, and short answer essays—and get many helpful tips on writing your own.

College Board: Essays
https://bigfuture.collegeboard.org/get-in/essays
The College Board offers this library of articles, videos, and slideshows that give sound advice on writing application essays.

Apprenticeship Programs ··

CareerOneStop: Apprenticeship Program Locator
http://maps.servicelocator.org/education/apprenticeship.aspx
The U.S. Department of Labor provides this database of apprenticeship programs that you can search by city and state or zip code to find apprenticeship programs near you.

The 21st Century Registered Apprenticeship Community of Practice
https://21stcenturyapprenticeship.workforce3one.org
Learn about apprenticeship programs on this website, designed to create a community of apprentices, apprenticeship sponsors, and others interested in apprenticeship programs. You will find news, videos, job advice and postings, and some encouraging apprenticeship success stories here. There are also discussion boards in case you have a question for the apprenticeship community.

Unions.org
www.unions.org
Find trade unions in your area that sponsor apprenticeship programs.

U.S. Office of Apprenticeship
The Office of Apprenticeship offers users several ways to find registered apprenticeships:

> Registered Apprenticeship Program Sponsors Database: http://oa.doleta.gov/bat.cfm?start
> List of State Apprenticeship Websites: www.doleta.gov/oa/sainformation.cfm
> State Offices of Apprenticeship: www.doleta.gov/oa/stateoffices.cfm

U.S. Office of Apprenticeship List of Apprenticeable Occupations
www.doleta.gov/oa/occupations.cfm.
Read through this extensive list to see the wide range of apprenticeable occupations.

Associate Degree Programs ·····································

CareerOneStop: Education and Training Finder
www.careerinfonet.org/edutraining
The U.S. Department of Labor offers this detailed database of educational programs, including associate degree programs. You can search for programs by occupation, institution name, or degree and see a list of schools in your area that offer what you're looking for.

College Navigator
http://nces.ed.gov/collegenavigator
This is probably the most useful website on the Internet for both finding a school and discovering how much it will cost. From the main page, you can choose your state, what level of credential you're looking to earn (certificate, associate degree, etc.), your program (you can browse available programs), what kind of institution you'd like to attend (less-than-two-year, two-year, etc.), and many more options in the search menu. Your search results will be a list of institutions that fulfill all of your criteria, and you can click on each one and receive detailed information on costs, enrollment, and programs of study offered. The site is sponsored by the U.S. Department of Education, so everything on the site is free.

Career and Skills Assessment Tests ······················

Career Key
www.careerkey.org
The Career Key test links personality traits to career characteristics and is used frequently to help people figure out what they will be good at. Test-takers are categorized into six career types and matched to their ideal work environment types. There is a fee to take this test.

Career Perfect
www.careerperfect.com/content/career-planning-free-tests
Career Perfect offers several good, free tests that help with career planning, including a work values inventory and a work preference inventory.

LiveCareer

www.livecareer.com/career-test

LiveCareer offers interest inventories and other tests that may help if you don't know exactly what you want to do for a career. You may have to click past educational opportunities LiveCareer tries to offer you, but the tests are informative.

Myers-Briggs Type Indicator

www.mbticomplete.com

Myers-Briggs is a classic and widely used test that classifies test-takers into one of sixteen personality types based on four fundamental traits. There is a fee to take this test.

O*NET Career Exploration Tools

www.onetcenter.org

O*NET offers a set of self-directed career exploration and assessment tools for "students who are exploring the school-to-work transition." These tools are designed to help people discover what they like to do, what is important to them in their working life, and what they do well. One of the main advantages of the tools is that users can link their results directly to occupational information in O*NET's database of more than 900 occupations to create a list of potentially compatible careers.

> ▸ The **Interest Profiler** is a career interest assessment tool that promotes self-knowledge about career interests, fosters career awareness, and directly links the user to a list of potential careers. You can download the software for the computerized version at www.onetcenter.org/CIP.html or complete a shortened version online at www.mynextmove.org/explore/ip.
> ▸ The **Work Importance Profiler** identifies work preferences and values that are important to you. After you input the level of education, training, and experience you currently have or expect to have, the computer generates the Occupations Report, a list of occupations whose important work preferences and values correspond with yours. Download this assessment at www.onet center.org/WIP.html.

Because these tools were developed by the U.S. Department of Labor, they are free to use.

Strong Interest Inventory

The Strong Interest Inventory, one of the most popular career self-assessment tools, is designed to help people make career and educational plans. Your high school counselor or local community college career counselor is bound to have it, or you can purchase it online on several websites.

Career Counseling

National Board for Certified Counselors (NBCC): Counselor Finder
www.nbcc.org/counselorfind
Verify the credentials of a career counselor or find one in your area with this tool from the NBCC.

One-Stop Career Center Locator
www.servicelocator.org/onestopcenters.asp
Locate a One-Stop Career Center near you where you can receive one-on-one career counseling. One-Stop Career Centers are sponsored by the U.S. Department of Labor, so all services provided there are free.

Career Exploration

Books

Bolles, Richard N. *What Color Is Your Parachute? 2013: A Practical Manual for Job-Hunters and Career-Changers.* Berkeley, CA: Ten Speed Press, 2012.

Christen, Carol, and Richard N. Bolles, *What Color Is Your Parachute? for Teens: Discovering Yourself, Defining Your Future,* 2nd ed. Berkeley, CA: Ten Speed Press, 2010.

Jansen, Julie. *I Don't Know What I Want, but I Know It's Not This: A Step-by-Step Guide to Finding Gratifying Work,* rev. ed. New York: Penguin, 2010.

Lore, Nicholas. *The Pathfinder: How to Choose or Change Your Career for a Lifetime of Satisfaction and Success,* revised and updated. New York: Touchstone, 2012.

Sturman, Gerald M. *If You Knew Who You Were, You Could Be Who You Are*. Bedford, NY: Bierman House, 2010.

Tieger, Paul D., and Barbara Barron-Tieger. *Do What You Are: Discover the Perfect Career for You through the Secrets of Personality Type*. New York: Little, Brown and Company, 2007.

Websites

America's Career Infonet
www.careerinfonet.org
The main page is full of links to great information for people exploring careers. Click on any of them for information and tools to help you zoom in from the big picture, including information specific to the state where you live or want to move to, and view videos on nearly 550 occupations. This site is sponsored by the U.S. Department of Labor, so all of the information is free.

ExploreHEALTHCareers.org: Career Explorer
http://explorehealthcareers.org/en/careers
According to its website, the mission of ExploreHEALTHCareers.org is "to help solve two urgent problems in American healthcare: the underrepresentation of minorities in the workforce, and the lack of health professionals in medically underserved communities." The website provides detailed, up-to-date profiles of 118 health professions, which represent all levels of education and training.

Exploring Career Information
www.bls.gov/k12
The U.S. Bureau of Labor Statistics offers this great job portal for high school students and graduates. The site, geared at high schoolers, lists careers by personal interest category: math, reading, science, social studies, music and arts, building and fixing things, helping people, computers, law, managing money, sports, nature, and more.

MyFuture.com
www.myfuture.com
Check out career-planning tools for young adults thinking about their next steps. Because this site was produced by the U.S. Department of Defense,

it is particularly informative about careers in military service. One tool on this website, MyPathway, will lead you through the decision-making process of finding a career and training for that career.

My Next Move

www.mynextmove.org

This site asks, "What do you want to do for a living?" and offers three ways to answer:

> ▸ **"I want to be a . . ."** If you know what you'd like to do for a living, you can "describe your dream career in a few words" in the blank provided, click Search, and you will be taken to a list of jobs that are relevant.
> ▸ **"I'll know it when I see it."** Click on a pull-down menu, select from a list of industries, and click Browse to explore occupations by the industry you want to be in.
> ▸ **"I'm not really sure."** Click Start to answer a series of questions to help guide you to information on careers you might be interested in. Based on your answers, you'll receive a list of suggested careers that match your interests and training.

One of the great features of this site is the simple and user-friendly occupation profile pages. My Next Move is sponsored by the U.S. Department of Labor, so all of the information and tools are free.

Occupational Outlook Handbook (OOH)

www.bls.gov/ooh

There are a variety of excellent resources available from the Bureau of Labor Statistics, and this is one of the best. The OOH lists hundreds of careers along with career outlook, wages, and the education and training needed to be hired in that career.

O*NET Online

www.onetonline.org

O*NET Online is an interactive website for exploring jobs and job trends. It's particularly useful because you can search for occupations by skills, tools, and technology. The information on this site is free.

QVerus
www.pathbuilder.com
Formerly Pathbuilder, QVerus is a career exploration website that shows real people in real jobs, through interviews with them and profiles of them.

Certificate Programs

America's CareerInfonet Certificate Finder
www.acinet.org/certifications_new
This U.S. Department of Labor database can be searched by industry, occupation, and location to pinpoint certificate programs.

College Navigator
http://nces.ed.gov/collegenavigator
This is probably the most useful website on the Internet for both finding a school and discovering how much it will cost. From the main page, you can choose your state, what level of credential you're looking to earn (certificate, associate degree, etc.), your program (you can browse available programs), what kind of institution you'd like to attend (less-than-two-year, two-year, etc.), and many more options in the search menu. Your search results will be a list of institutions that fulfill all of your criteria, and you can click on each one and receive detailed information on costs, enrollment, and programs of study offered. It is sponsored by the U.S. Department of Education, so everything on the site is free.

U.S. Armed Forces Credentialing Opportunities Online (COOL)
www.cool.navy.mil, www.cool.army.mil
These websites explain how military personnel can meet civilian certification and license requirements related to their Military Occupational Specialty (MOS). It also links to programs that will provide that certification and licensing.

Costs, Education, and Training

College Affordability and Transparency Center
http://collegecost.ed.gov/catc
This handy website, sponsored by the U.S. Department of Education, provides real costs of attending real schools, along with estimated yearly

living expenses for students while attending. There is a section for estimating total costs of career and vocational programs.

College Navigator

http://nces.ed.gov/collegenavigator

This is probably the most useful website on the Internet for finding a school and discovering how much it will cost. From the main page, you can choose your state, what level of credential you're looking to earn (certificate, associate degree, etc.), your program (you can browse available programs), what kind of institution you'd like to attend (less-than-two-year, two-year, etc.), and many more options in the search menu. Your search results will be a list of institutions that fulfill all of your criteria, and you can click on each one and receive detailed information on costs, enrollment, and programs of study offered. It is sponsored by the U.S. Department of Education, so everything on the site is free.

Disabled Workers

Disability.gov

www.disability.gov

This award-winning website is a comprehensive database of disability-related resources in communities nationwide. It is sponsored by the U.S. Department of Labor's Office of Disability Employment Policy, but the resources it lists aren't limited to federal services and programs; there are state and local services and programs as well. To find career resources in your community, click the Employment button on the main page.

Job Accommodation Network (JAN)

http://askjan.org
800-526-7234 (voice); 877-781-9403 (TTY)
Visit this website for information on workplace accommodations for people with disabilities.

National Federation of the Blind (NFB)

www.nfb.org/working
410-659-9314
The NFB offers valuable resources for blind job seekers.

National Organization on Disability
www.nod.org/economic
646-505-1191; info@nod.org
The National Organization on Disability provides information on employment opportunities, transportation, and other considerations for people
with a wide variety of disabilities.

Education Tax Credits and Deductions

American Opportunity Tax Credit: Questions and Answers
www.irs.gov/uac/American-Opportunity-Tax-Credit:-Questions-and
-Answers
Learn more about this tax credit targeting low- and middle-income students.

IRS Publications: Lifetime Learning Credit
www.irs.gov/publications/p970/ch03.html
The Lifetime Learning Tax Credit is available for all years of postsecondary education and for courses to acquire or improve job skills. The qualifying student does not need to be pursuing a degree or other recognized
education credential. For details, visit this IRS website.

Tax Benefits for Education: Information Center
You may be able to take deductions on tuition and fees. You can get an
overview of all of your tax options for education at this IRS website.

Tax Topics: Student Loan Interest Deduction
www.irs.gov/taxtopics/tc456.html
Interest payments on student loans may be eligible for a tax deduction.
See this IRS website for details.

Federal Financial Aid, General

Completing the FAFSA
http://studentaid.ed.gov/sites/default/files/2012-13-completing-the-fafsa.pdf
The FAFSA is a long form that can be complicated to fill out. This publication, available for download online, will guide you through the process.

FAFSA4caster

www.fafsa4caster.ed.gov

If you're not ready to fill out and submit your FAFSA, you can use this website to get an estimate of the kinds of financial aid you might qualify for.

Federal Student Aid Gateway

http://studentaid.ed.gov

This website directs you to up-to-date information on all types of financial aid offered by the federal government.

Federal Student Aid Information Center (FSAIC)

1-800-4-FED-AID (1-800-433-3243); 1-800-730-8913 (TTY)

The staff at the FSAIC can answer many of your financial aid questions, including these:

> ▶ What kinds of financial aid does the federal government offer to students?
> ▶ How do I fill out my FAFSA?
> ▶ How can I correct errors on my Student Aid Report?
> ▶ When do I have to start repaying my federal loan?

Free Application for Federal Student Aid (FAFSA)

www.fafsa.ed.gov

You should begin your search for financial aid by filling out and submitting the FAFSA. The information you submit through the FAFSA will determine your expected family contribution, which will help determine the amount of financial aid you are eligible for. You must submit the FAFSA to be considered for federal, state, and most institutional aid.

Federal Government Jobs

USAJobs

www.usajobs.gov

Information on getting civilian positions within the federal government is available from the U.S. Office of Personnel Management through USA-Jobs, the federal government's official employment information system. Use it to locate and apply for federal job opportunities.

Federal Grants ···

Federal Supplemental Educational Opportunity Grants (FSEOG)
http://studentaid.ed.gov/types/grants-scholarships/fseog
In order to receive this grant, you must be eligible for a Pell Grant and have exceptional financial need.

Iraq and Afghanistan Service Grant
http://studentaid.ed.gov/types/grants-scholarships/iraq-afghanistan-service
This grant is for students not eligible for a Pell Grant (only because of that program's need requirements) and whose parent or guardian died as a result of military service in Iraq or Afghanistan after September 11, 2001.

Pell Grants
http://studentaid.ed.gov/types/grants-scholarships/pell
Pell Grants are awarded to students based on need. To receive a Pell Grant, you must be an undergraduate or vocational student who does not have a bachelor's or a professional degree.

Federal Student Loan Repayment ·····························
and Forgiveness

Income-Based Repayment Plan (IBR)
www.ibrinfo.org
To ease the economic hardship of many people paying back federal loans, Congress passed the College Cost Reduction and Access Act of 2007. For most eligible borrowers, IBR loan payments will be less than 10 percent of their income. IBR will also forgive any remaining debt after twenty-five years of qualifying payments.

Public Service Loan Forgiveness Program
www.studentaid.ed.gov/publicservice
The College Cost Reduction and Access Act of 2007 also offers forgiveness for outstanding Federal Direct loans for borrowers who make 120 qualifying payments while working full-time in a public service job. Federal, state, and local government jobs qualify for this program, as well as many jobs in the nonprofit sector.

Federal Student Loans ....

Direct PLUS Loans for Parents
http://studentaid.ed.gov/types/loans/plus
Parents (biological or adoptive), or stepparents, in some cases, of dependent students may apply for a Direct PLUS loan to help pay for a child's education expenses. Read more about it here.

Direct Loans
http://studentaid.ed.gov/types/loans/subsidized-unsubsidized
Direct loans are low-interest loans for eligible recipients to help cover the cost of education at a college or university, community college, or trade, career, or technical school. Direct loans can be subsidized or unsubsidized.

Federal Student Aid: Perkins Loans
http://studentaid.ed.gov/types/loans/perkins
Perkins loans are low-interest loans offered to full- or part-time students with exceptional need.

Franchise Ownership ....

Introduction to Franchising
http://sba.frannet.com
This free online course cosponsored by the U.S. Small Business Administration and FranNet walks you through the process of buying, running, and marketing a franchise.

Small Business Information Center: Franchise
www.sbdcnet.org/small-business-information-center/franchise
Visit this SBDCNet website for useful franchising tools and information.

Federal Trade Commission, Bureau of Consumer Protection: Business Center
http://business.ftc.gov/selected-industries/franchises-and-business-opportunities
The Business Center of the Federal Trade Commission offers resources to help people spot business opportunities and investment scams and avoid common franchising mistakes.

Interviewing

Books

Beshara, Tony. *Acing the Interview: How to Ask and Answer the Questions That Will Get You the Job.* New York: AMACOM, 2008.

Burns, Dan. *The First 60 Seconds: Win the Job Interview before It Begins.* Naperville, IL: Sourcebooks, 2009.

Oliver, Vicky. *301 Smart Answers to Tough Interview Questions.* Naperville, IL: Sourcebooks, 2005.

Schuman, Nancy. *The Job Interview Phrase Book: The Things to Say to Get You the Job You Want.* Avon, MA: Adams Media, 2009.

Job Search, General

Books

Bolles, Mark Emery, and Richard Nelson Bolles. *What Color Is Your Parachute? Guide to Job-Hunting Online: Career Sites, Gateways, Getting Interviews, Job Search Engines, Mobile Apps, Networking, Niche Sites, Posting Resumes, Research Sites, Super Sites, and More,* 6th ed. Berkeley, CA: Ten Speed Press, 2011.

Doyle, Alison. *Internet Your Way to a New Job: How to Really Find a Job Online,* 3rd ed. Cupertino, CA: Happy About, 2011.

Editors of the American Library Association. *How to Get a Great Job: A Library How-To Handbook.* Chicago: American Library Association, 2011.

Levinson, Jay Conrad, and David E. Perry. *Guerrilla Marketing for Job Hunters 3.0: How to Stand Out from the Crowd and Tap Into the Hidden Job Market Using Social Media and 999 Other Tactics Today.* Hoboken, NJ: John Wiley and Sons, 2011.

Shapiro, Cynthia. *What Does Somebody Have to Do to Get a Job Around Here? 44 Insider Secrets That Will Get You Hired.* New York: St. Martin's Griffin, 2008.

Whitcomb, Susan Britton. *Job Search Magic: Insider Secrets from America's Career and Life Coach.* Indianapolis, IN: JIST Works, 2006.

Yate, Martin. *Knock 'Em Dead 2013: The Ultimate Job Search Guide.* Avon, MA: Adams Media, 2012.

Websites

Job-Hunt
www.job-hunt.org
Visit Job-Hunt for job search information and links to useful job sites.

Quintessential Careers
www.quintcareers.com
Quintessential Careers is a job search engine with resources for job seekers.

The Riley Guide
www.rileyguide.com
While the design of this website may not be beautiful, the information collected here is valuable to job seekers.

WetFeet
www.wetfeet.com
This is a great site for first-time job seekers.

Military Student Aid

Aid for Military Families
www.studentaid.ed.gov/military
This page provides a good overview of the financial aid options for military families.

Iraq and Afghanistan Service Grant
http://studentaid.ed.gov/types/grants-scholarships/iraq-afghanistan-service
This grant is for students not eligible for a Pell Grant (only because of that program's need requirements) and whose parent or guardian died as a result of military service in Iraq or Afghanistan after September 11, 2001.

Military.com: Scholarship Finder
http://aid.military.com/scholarship/search-for-scholarships.do
Search a large database of grants and scholarships available to those in the military community.

The Post-9/11 GI Bill
www.gibill.va.gov/benefits/post_911_gibill
This bill provides financial support for education and housing to people who served in the military for a specified amount of time after September 10, 2001. You must have received an honorable discharge to be eligible.

Reserve Educational Assistance Program (REAP)
www.gibill.va.gov/benefits/other_programs/reap.html
This is an education benefit program designed to provide educational assistance to members of the reserve components of the military called or ordered to active duty in response to a war or national emergency. Certain reservists who were activated during a specified amount of time after September 11, 2001, are either eligible for education benefits or eligible for increased benefits.

Survivors & Dependents Assistance (DEA)
www.gibill.va.gov/benefits/other_programs/dea.html
DEA provides education and training opportunities to eligible dependents of certain veterans. The benefits can be used for degree and certificate programs, apprenticeships, and on-the-job training.

Networking

Books

Benjamin, Susan. *Perfect Phrases for Professional Networking: Hundreds of Ready-to-Use Phrases for Meeting and Keeping Helpful Contacts—Everywhere You Go.* New York: McGraw-Hill, 2009.

Crompton, Diane, and Ellen Sautter. *Find a Job through Social Networking: Use LinkedIn, Twitter, Facebook, Blogs, and More to Advance Your Career.* Indianapolis, IN: JIST Works, 2010.

Hansen, Katharine. *A Foot in the Door: Networking Your Way into the Hidden Job Market.* Berkeley, CA: Ten Speed Press, 2008.

Jacoway, Kristen. *I'm in a Job Search—Now What??? Using LinkedIn, Facebook, and Twitter as Part of Your Job Search Strategy,* 2nd ed. Cupertino, CA: Happy About, 2012.

Levinson, Jay Conrad, and Monroe Mann. *Guerrilla Networking: A Proven Battle Plan to Attract the Very People You Want to Meet.* Bloomington, IN: AuthorHouse, 2009.

Mckay, Harvey. *Dig Your Well before You're Thirsty: The Only Networking Book You'll Ever Need.* New York: Currency Books, 1999.

Pierson, Orville. *Highly Effective Networking: Meet the Right People and Get a Great Job.* Pompton Plains, NJ: Career Press, 2009.

Sheridan, Valerie S., Madiha Waris Qureshi, Charles Slife, and David Epstein. *Directory of National Trade and Professional Associations 2011*. Bethesda, MD: Columbia Books, 2011.

Vermeiren, Jan. *How to REALLY Use LinkedIn*, 2nd ed. Charleston, SC: CreateSpace, 2009.

Online Colleges and Universities

The Database of Accredited Postsecondary Institutions and Programs

http://ope.ed.gov/accreditation

Online colleges and universities cover most of the same material as their traditional classroom counterparts, but they offer classes over the Internet. Before you apply to an online program, use this resource to verify that it is accredited.

Researching Companies

Glassdoor

www.glassdoor.com

This is good website to use if you want the inside scoop on working for a certain company. Employees and former employees post reviews of companies here and rate them on work environment, leadership, and other qualities. Many of these reviews contain content or opinions you may not want to share with your potential employer during a job interview.

Hoover's

www.hoovers.com
To research companies using this site, you will have to pay for a subscription. Your local library may already have a subscription to this service, so consult a librarian.

Quintessential Careers: Guide to Researching Companies, Industries, and Countries

www.quintcareers.com/researching_companies
This page provides very useful links to resources you can use to research any company you are interested in working for or have an interview with.

The Riley Guide: How to Research Employers

www.rileyguide.com/employer.html
The Riley Guide provides links to sources for researching companies.

Vault: Employer Reviews

www.vault.com/wps/portal/usa/companies
In the Employer Reviews section, Vault provides uncensored reviews posted by employees and former employees. You may not want to share this information in an interview setting.

Resources and Cover Letters

Books

Betrus, Michael. *202 Great Cover Letters*. New York: McGraw-Hill, 2007.

Dikel, Margaret, and Frances Roehm. *The Guide to Internet Job Searching*. New York: McGraw-Hill, 2008.

Enelow, Wendy, and Louise Kursmark. *Cover Letter Magic,* 4th ed. Indianapolis, IN: JIST Works, 2010.

Ireland, Susan. *The Complete Idiot's Guide to the Perfect Resume,* 5th ed. New York: Alpha Books, 2010.

Schultze, Quentin J., with a foreword by Richard N. Bolles. *Resume 101: A Student and Recent-Grad Guide to Crafting Resumes and Cover Letters That Land Jobs.* Berkeley, CA: Ten Speed Press, 2011.

Whitcomb, Susan Britton. *Resume Magic,* 4th ed. St. Paul, MN: JIST Works, 2010.

Yate, Martin. *Knock 'Em Dead Cover Letters,* 10th ed. Avon, MA: Adams Media, 2012.

Websites

The Damn Good Resume Website
www.damngood.com
If you want to look at sample resumes from a wide variety of jobs, this is the website for you. Author Yana Parker provides information about resume content and format as well as excellent advice about dealing with resume problems such as many short-term jobs or a long gap between jobs.

Dummies.com: Resumes
www.dummies.com/how-to/business-careers/careers/Resumes.html
If you need to figure out which type of resume structure will work best for you and your goals, this is the place to find worthwhile descriptions and samples of the most common, including various hybrids. The site also tackles questions about video resumes, portfolio resumes, and keyword resumes.

The Riley Guide: Help with Your Resume and CV
www.rileyguide.com/resprep.html
This site lists links to dozens of other sites that offer resume tips and advice as well as information about interviewing and how resume readers deal with and react to actual resumes.

WetFeet
www.wetfeet.com/advice-tools/resume-cover-letter
Career-advice company WetFeet offers tips on all kinds of resumes, including advice on how to deliver a "perfect" electronic resume.

Salary Negotiation

Books

Fisher, Roger, William L. Ury, and Bruce Patton. *Getting to Yes: Negotiating Agreement without Giving In,* rev. ed. New York: Penguin, 2011.

Miller, Lee E. *Get More Money on Your Next Job . . . in Any Economy.* New York: McGraw-Hill, 2009.

Pinkley, Robin L., and Gregory B. Northcraft. *Get Paid What You're Worth: The Expert Negotiators' Guide to Salary and Compensation.* New York: St. Martin's Griffin, 2003.

Wegerbauer, Maryanne. *Next-Day Salary Negotiation: Prepare Tonight to Get Your Best Pay Tomorrow.* Indianapolis, IN: JIST Works, 2007.

Websites

Glassdoor
www.glassdoor.com
This website gives you the scoop on what people are making in certain occupations and at particular companies.

PayScale.com
www.payscale.com
If you want to get an idea what others are making in the occupation you are interested in, visit this website.

Quintessential Careers: Salary Negotiation and Job Offer Tools and Resources for Job-Seekers
www.quintcareers.com/salary_negotiation.html
Quintessential Careers offers some advice on how to negotiate your salary.

Saving for Education and Training ························

College Savings Plan Network (CSPN)
www.collegesavings.org
As the CSPN website points out, "Section 529 college savings plans have been wildly successful in motivating parents to invest and save for a child's higher education expenses." The wide range of features in the many 529 plans offered can be confusing, however. CSPN lets you compare 529 plans by state and feature.

IRS Coverdell Education Savings Account (ESA)
www.irs.gov/publications/p970/ch07.html
Read more about Coverdell ESAs, which were created as an incentive to help parents and students save for educational expenses.

Treasury Direct: Savings Bonds and Education Planning
www.treasurydirect.gov/indiv/planning/plan_education.htm
U.S. savings bonds have been the go-to graduation gift for many years, but the Series EE and Series I bonds can be used to pay for college. The Education Savings Bond Program makes these bonds tax-free when they are used to pay for college expenses or rolled over into a 529 savings plan.

Scholarship Applications ························

College Board: How to Apply for a Scholarship
https://bigfuture.collegeboard.org/pay-for-college/scholarships-and
-grants/how-to-apply-for-a-college-scholarship
The College Board website has an entire section about grants and scholarships, including this article, which is a useful overview of the application process.

Scholarships.com: Scholarship Application Strategies
www.scholarships.com/financial-aid/college-scholarships/
scholarship-application-strategies
This page from Scholarships.com offers helpful strategies for applying for scholarships.

Scholarships ···

Books

The College Board. *Scholarship Handbook 2013*. New York: College
Board, 2012. (A new edition is published every year.)

Tanabe, Gen, and Kelly Tanabe. *The Ultimate Scholarship Book 2013*.
Belmont, CA: SuperCollege, LLC, 2012. (A new edition is published every year.)

Websites

College Board: Bigfuture Scholarship Search
https://bigfuture.collegeboard.org/scholarship-search
Use this College Board website to find scholarships and other financial
aid, as well as internships, from more than 2,200 programs.

Fastweb Scholarships
www.fastweb.com/college-scholarships
This free website offers a searchable database of more than 1.5 million
scholarships.

Military.com: Scholarship Finder
http://aid.military.com/scholarship/search-for-scholarships.do
If you are a member of the military community, you will want to search
this free database for scholarships.

Sallie Mae's Scholarship Search
http://go.salliemae.com/scholarship
This free site provides an extensive, up-to-date database of more than 3
million scholarships, which you can search using many different criteria.

Scholarships.com
www.scholarships.com
Scholarship.com offers a free database of more than 2.7 million local,
college, and national scholarships.

U.S. Department of Labor Scholarship Search
www.careerinfonet.org/scholarshipsearch

Small Business Information

Association of Small Business Development Centers
www.asbdc-us.org
Visit this website for all kinds of useful information on starting and own-ing your own business. You can also find a Small Business Development Center near you, where you can receive counseling, information, assis-tance, and training in starting and running a small business. Much of this help is free or very low cost.

Small Business Development Centers (SBDCs)
www.sba.gov/content/small-business-development-centers-sbdcs
If you want to start your own small business, this website should be your first stop.

U.S. Small Business Administration
www.sba.gov
Find information on starting a business, getting a loan, securing govern-ment contracts, and more. You can also find a district office near you where you can receive counseling, mentoring, and training.

Social Networking Savings Programs, Credit Card Rebates, and Loyalty Programs

GradeFund
www.gradefund.com
Here you can ask friends and family to sponsor certain educational bench-marks in your life. For example, you can ask them to pledge a certain amount for each A you receive. The site allows you to post your grades.

GradSave
www.gradsave.com
This website serves as a "gift registry" for college savings. Register, and link the account to your 529 savings plan; any funds contributed will go

directly into your 529 account. Use social media to invite friends and family to contribute to your college savings.

Upromise
www.upromise.com
When you use your Upromise cards to buy certain products or buy from certain stores, a rebate is sent to the college fund of your choice. Upromise has one of the biggest networks of retailers, and it was recently purchased by student loan giant Sallie Mae.

State Grants

U.S. Department of Education's List of State Grant Agencies
http://wdcrobcolp01.ed.gov/Programs/EROD/org_list.cfm?category_cd=SGT
Here you will find a list of individual state agencies that provide grants for education and worker training, along with their websites and contact information. Often, the website for the grant agency in your state lists all grants available to you.

Index

NOTE: Italicized *t* next to page locators indicates tables or text outside the main content.

A

Accreditation Council for Occupational Therapy Education, 70
administrative assistants, careers as, 29–31
admissions essay, 89–93
Air-Conditioning, Heating, and Refrigeration Institute (certification), 57
Air Force, careers in, 42–45
American Opportunity Tax Credit, 129*t*
America's Career Infonet (career database), 9
appearance, interviews and, 121*t*
applications
    elements of, 85–86
    essay, 89–93
    fees, 86
    form components, 86–87
    tracker (form), 95*t*–96*t*
    transcripts and test scores, 87
apprenticeships
    carpenters, 50–51
    chefs and head cooks, 52–53
    masonry, 51–52
    plumbers, pipefitters, steamfitters, 49–50
    program benefits, 75–78

armed forces, careers in, 42–45
Armed Services Vocational Aptitude Battery (ASVAB), 43
Army, careers in, 42–45
arts, careers in, 25–27
assessment tests, 11–13, 119
associate degrees (careers)
    dental hygienists, 70–71
    diagnostic medical sonographers, 71–73
    funeral service managers, 65–67
    occupational therapist assistants, 69–70
    paralegals and legal assistants, 67–68
    respiratory therapists, 68–69
attachments, e-resumes and, 106

B

bartering for classes, 81
blockmasons, apprenticeships, 51–52
Bolles, Richard, 4–5, 112
books and supplies, costs, 126
brainstorming, essays and, 91
brickmasons, apprenticeships, 51–52
business, starting, 20–22, 82–84

C

cancellation (financial aid term), 142
capitalizing the loan (financial aid term), 142

Career Interest Inventory, 17–18
Career Key (assessment), 12
career objectives, resumes and, 100
Career Perfect (assessment), 13
career planning, 1–18
Career Programs Assessment (CPAt), 87
careers
    counselors for, 2–4
    databases of, 5–9
    fastest growing, 9–11
    interests tests for, 11–13
    See also jobs
careers without training
    franchise owner, 23
    sales jobs, 23–25
    small business owner, 20–22
    visual and performing artists, 25–27
cargo agents, careers as, 28–29
carpenters, apprenticeships, 50–51
certification, locating programs, 78–79
certified careers
    court reporters, 60–61
    defined, 55
    HVAC technicians, 56–57
    licensed practical and vocational
        nurses, 63–64
    sound engineering technicians, 61–63
    surgical technologists, 59–60
chefs, careers as, 52–54
Christen, Carol, 5
chronological resumes, 97
claims adjusters, careers as, 38
claims appraisers, careers as, 38
claims examiners, careers as, 38
claims investigators, careers as, 38
classes, finding, 80–84
The College Application Essay (McGinty),
    90*t*
College Board Scholarship Search
    (scholarship website), 137
College Board (website), 92*t*
College Cost Reduction and Access Act,
    140*t*
College View (scholarship website), 137
CollegeNet.com (scholarship website), 137
Commission on Accreditation of Allied
    Health Education Programs, 59–60
communication access real-time
    translation (CART), 61
community centers, classes and, 84

community colleges, classes and, 83
*The Complete Idiot's Guide to the Perfect
    Resume* (Ireland), 107*t*
Computer-Adaptive Placement
    Assessment and Support System
    (COMPASS), 87
computer classes, 83–84
cooks, apprenticeships, 52–53
correctional officers, careers as, 31–33
costs. *see* funding training and education
counselors, career, 2–4
court clerks, careers as, 35
court reporters, careers as, 60–61
Coverdell Education Savings Accounts, 128
credentials, 55–64
credit card rebates, funding education and,
    128–129
credit check (financial aid term), 142

D

The Damn Good Resume Website
    (website), 104*t*
dancers, careers as, 26–27
data release number (financial aid term),
    142
debt, student, vii–viii
deductions and tax credits, education, 129*t*
deferment (financial aid term), 142
dental hygienists, careers as, 70–71
diagnostic medical sonographers, careers
    as, 71–73
digital audio recording technology
    (DART), 60
Dikel, Margaret, 107*t*
Direct PLUS loans, 140–141
disbursement (financial aid term), 143
dispatchers, careers as, 33–34
dispensing opticians, careers as, 40
drug tests, 119
Dummies.com Resumes (website), 104*t*

E

e-mailing resumes, 105–106
education
    certification, 55–64
    expenses for, 125–127
    formal training, 41–54
    on-the-job training, 19–54
    paying for, 125–150
    personal resources, 127–130

taking classes, 80–84
where to look, 75–84
embalmers, careers as, 66
emergency medical technician (EMT), 46
entrepreneurs, business and, 22
essays, how to, 85–96
expected family contribution (financial aid term), 143
extracurricular activities, resumes and, 100

F
FAFSA (financial aid), 131–132, 134*t*, 143
Fastweb (scholarship website), 137
federal job programs, 3–4
federal methodology (financial aid term), 143
Federal Supplemental Educational Opportunity Grant (FSEOG), 133–134
federal work-study (FWS), 138
fees, applications and, 86
financial aid
    applying for, 130–132
    deadlines, 134*t*
    FAFSA, 131–132, 134*t*, 143
    grants, 132–135
    loans, 139–142
    scholarships, 135–138
    work-study, 138
financial need (financial aid term), 143
firefighters, careers as, 45–47
FireRecruit.com (website), 47
529 savings plan, 127–128
follow-up interviews, 116–117
forbearance (financial aid term), 143
formal training (careers)
    armed forces, 42–45
    firefighters, 45–47
    police and sheriff officers, 47–49
formatting e-resumes, 101–104
401(k) plans (funding education), 130
franchise, buying, 23
free classes, locating, 80–81
freight agents, careers as, 28–29
functional resumes, 98
funding training and education
    costs of, 125–127
    financial aid, 130–141

glossary of terms, 142–144
grants, 132–135
loans, 139–142
personal resources for, 127–130
scholarships, 135–138
work-study, 138
funeral directors, careers as, 65–67
funeral service managers, careers as, 65–67

G
GradeFund (funding education), 128
GradSave (funding education), 128
grants (financial aid), 132–135, 143
    personal inventory, 145*t*–148*t*
green jobs, 11*t*
group interviews, 117
The Guide to Internet Job Searching (Dikel and Roehm), 107*t*

H
head cooks, apprenticeships, 52–53
hearing impaired, working with, 61
high school counselors, 2
home equity line of credit (funding education), 130
honors, listing on resume, 100
How to Get a Great Job (ALA), 116–117
HVAC technicians, 56–57

I
If You Knew Who You Were, You Could Be Who You Are (Sturman), 4
in-person interviews, 115–116
Income-Based Repayment Plan, 140*t*
interest rate (financial aid term), 143
interests, findings personal, 1–18
interviews
    basics of, 113*t*
    checklist for, 123
    informational, 14–15, 112–114
    post-interview, 119–122
    preparation, 116*t*
    tracking sheet, 124*t*
    types of, 111–117
    what to say, 117–118
inventories, personal, 11–13, 17–18
Iraq and Afghanistan Service Grant, 133
Ireland, Susan, 107*t*

J

jailers, careers as, 31–33
job centers, classes and, 84
job outlooks
  associate degrees and, 74*t*
  certification and, 58*t*
  long-term on-the-job training and, 37*t*
  moderate-term on-the-job training
      and, 32*t*
  short-term on-the-job training and, 30*t*
job programs, local and federal, 3–4
jobs
  associate degree and, 65–74
  certification and, 55–64
  exploring interests and, 1–18
  formal training and, 41–54
  no formal training and, 19–40
  See also careers

L

legal assistants, careers as, 67–68
letters of recommendation, 88–89
libraries, classes and, 84
licensed practical and vocational nurses,
    careers as, 63–64
Lifetime Learning Credit, 129*t*
LiveCareer (assessment), 13
loans (funding education), 139–142
local job programs, 3–4
long-term on-the-job training (careers)
    claims adjusters, appraisers,
        examiners, and investigators, 38
    dispensing opticians, 40
    purchasing agents, 36
    water and wastewater treatment plant
        and system operators, 39
loyalty programs, funding education and,
    128–129

M

Marines, careers in, 42–45
McGinty, Sarah Myers, 90*t*
McGraw-Hill's Big Red Book of Resumes,
    107*t*
meter readers, careers as, 29
military service grants, 133
military student aid, 133*t*
Military.com (scholarship website), 137
moderate-term on-the-job training (careers)
    correctional officers and jailers, 31–33

court clerks, 35
dispatchers, 33–34
pharmacy technicians, 34–35
Montgomery G.I. Bill, 133*t*
morticians, careers as, 65–67
musicians, careers as, 26–27
My Next Move (career database), 7
Myers-Briggs Type Indicator (assessment),
    11–12
MyFuture.com (career database), 9

N

National Association of Legal Assistants/
    Paralegals (NALA), 68
National Board for Certified Counselors, 3
National Council of State Boards of
    Nursing, 64
National Court Reporters Association, 61
National Federation of Licensed Practical
    Nurses, 64
National Occupational Competency
    Testing Institute (certification), 57
Navy, careers in, 42–45
needs assessment (financial aid term), 143
needs-based (financial aid term), 143
nonfederal grants, 134–135
nonverbal communication, interviews
    and, 118*t*
nurses, careers as, 63–64

O

Occupational Outlook Handbook (OOH)
    (career database), 5–7
occupational therapist assistants, careers
    as, 69–70
on-the-job-training
    careers with, 27–40
    formal training outlook, 44*t*
    long-term training outlook, 37*t*
    moderate-term training outlook, 32*t*
    short-term training outlook, 30*t*
O*NET Online (career database), 7–8,
    12–13
operating room technicians, careers as,
    59–60
opticians, careers as, 40

P

paralegals, careers as, 67–68
Pell grants (financial aid), 132–133

performing arts, careers in, 26–27
Perkins loans (funding education), 139
personal resources for education funding, 127–130
personality tests, 11–13
pharmacy technicians, careers as, 34–35
PIN (financial aid term), 143
pipefitters, apprenticeships, 49–50
plain text files, resumes and, 103
plumbers, apprenticeships, 49–50
police officers, careers as, 47–49
Post-9/11 GI Bill (financial aid), 133*t*
Postal Service mail carriers, careers as, 27–28
Public Service Loan Forgiveness program, 140*t*
purchasing agents, careers as, 36

Q

questions, sample informational interview, 15
QuintCareers (website), 92*t*

R

radio stations, careers in, 61–62
recommendations, letters of, 88–89
Registered Apprenticeship Program, 76–78
repayment plan, 140*t*
repayment schedule (financial aid term), 143
research, career planning and, 4–9
Reserve Educational Assistance Program (financial aid), 133*t*
residence costs, 126
respiratory therapists, careers as, 68–69
Resume Magic (Whitcomb), 107*t*
Resume 101 (Schultze), 107*t*
resume websites, 104*t*
resumes
    anatomy of, 98–101
    checklist worksheet, 109*t*–110*t*
    common mistakes, 107–108
    e-mailing, 105–106
    e-resumes, 101–105
    types of, 97–98
    version tracking worksheet, 110*t*
retirement plans (funding education), 130
The Riley Guide (website), 104*t*
Roehm, Frances, 107*t*

S

sales jobs, 23–25
Sallie Mae's Scholarship Search (scholarship website), 137
savings, funding education and, 127–130
savings bonds (funding education), 129–130
The Scholarship Handbook 2013 (College Board), 137
scholarship inventory, 145*t*–148*t*
Scholarships.com (scholarship website), 137
scholarships, 134–138, 143
Scholarships for Military Children (financial aid), 133*t*
Schultze, Quentin J., 107*t*
secretaries, careers as, 29–31
senior centers, classes and, 84
sheriff's patrol officer, careers as, 47–49
short-term on-the-job training (careers)
    cargo and freight agents, 28–29
    meter readers, 29
    postal service mail carriers, 27–28
    secretaries and administrative assistants, 29–31
signature page (financial aid term), 143
singers, careers as, 26–27
skills
    finding interests, 1–18
    resumes and, 100
    tests for, 119
Small Business Development Center (SBDC), 20–22, 80–83
social networking programs, education funding and, 128
Society of Broadcast Engineers, 63
sound engineering technicians, careers as, 61–63
steamfitters, apprenticeships, 49–50
stenographers, careers as, 60–61
stonemasons, apprenticeships, 51–52
Strong Interest Inventory (assessment), 12
student aid report (financial aid term), 144
student debt, vii–viii
Sturman, Gerald M., 4
subject lines, job e-mails and, 106
subsidized (financial aid term), 144
surgical technologists, careers as, 59–60
Survivors & Dependents Assistance (DEA) (financial aid), 133*t*

T

Tanabe, Gen, 137
Tanabe, Kelly, 137
tax credits and deductions for education, 129t, 141t
telephone interviews, 115
television stations, careers in, 61–62
test scores, applications and, 87
testing, interviews and, 119
thank-you notes, interviews and, 120, 122t
training
    certificate outlook, 58t
    costs and fees, 125–127
    formal training, 41–54
    formal training outlook, 44t
    long-term on-the-job training outlook, 37t
    moderate-term on-the-job training outlook, 32t
    paying for, 125–150
    personal resources to pay for, 127–130
    resources worksheet, 149t
    short-term on-the-job training outlook, 30t
    tracking form, 95t–96t
    where to find, 75–84
    without formal, 19–40
training and education programs, costs and fees, 125–127
transcripts, applications and, 87
travel, fees, 126
Treasury Direct (funding education), 130
typing tests, 119

U

The Ultimate Scholarship Book 2013 (Tanabe and Tanabe), 137
undertakers, careers as, 65–67
Upromise (funding education), 129

V

Veterans Educational Assistance Program (VEAP) (financial aid), 133t
visual arts, careers in, 25
volunteer work, resumes and, 99, 100

W

wastewater treatment plants, careers in, 39
water and wastewater treatment plant system operators, careers as, 39
water treatment plants, careers in, 39
What Color Is Your Parachute? (Bolles), 4
What Color Is Your Parachute? for Teens (Christen and Bolles), 5
work-study programs (financial aid), 138, 144
worksheets
    career interest inventory, 17t–18t
    interview tracking, 124t
    resumes, 109t–110t
    scholarships and grants, 145t–148t
    training/school application tracker, 95t–96t
    training and education resources, 149t